PRAISE F...
HOW TO SPEAK LIFE T...

Wives spend more time with their husb... ... ...yone else in their lives. Learning how to regulate your words to make the relationship be the most amazing it can be is an integral part of the marriage journey. Ann Wilson has taught me how to use my words as seeds and water them, as fire and stoke them, toward the growth of the marriage relationship. Our marriage is better, and I'm better as a result.

DAN ORLOVSKY, ESPN analyst;
former professional football player

Ann and Dave Wilson are the real deal. They vulnerably share the lessons they've learned from their mistakes and shortcomings to help other couples avoid heartache. Their balanced and authentic "tell it like it is" approach to marriage helps both husbands and wives feel seen and heard, but also connected and hopeful. This is the dose of hope your marriage needs.

DEBRA FILETA, M.A., LPC, counselor; bestselling author

Ann and Dave Wilson have been instrumental in the success of our marriage. They've given us the tools necessary to identify, address, and overcome everyday challenges that marriage brings—with wit when it's needed most. Even more importantly, they have given us practical ways of preventing issues before they arise. The Wilsons normalize the hard parts with humor and make us realize we aren't alone, no matter what chapter we're in.

BAKER AND EMILY MAYFIELD, NFL quarterback

Ann Wilson is one of my favorite people in the world, and I'm thrilled she has written this book. Her approach to this vital subject is kind yet piercing, full of strength yet full of grace and love. I know her message will be just as powerful generations from now, but I encourage you to read it *now*.

SHAUNTI FELDHAHN, social researcher; bestselling author,
For Women Only and *For Men Only*

I was a high school student at Dave and Ann Wilson's church, and I know firsthand how Ann's vulnerable storytelling gives way for others to find freedom and not make the same mistakes. Ann's storytelling is transformative. No matter what season your marriage is in, this all-encompassing guide will strengthen your heart and home. Read this book from cover to cover and discover your God-given superpowers as a wife.

ESTHER FLEECE ALLEN, bestselling author,
No More Faking Fine and *Your New Name*

Practically every woman reaches a stage in her marriage of disillusionment. Her husband isn't who she thought he was; the conflicts are deeper than she anticipated; romance is miles in the rearview mirror. This book will comfort you in knowing that you are not alone. But more than that, you will be encouraged with practical ways to change your mindset and infuse hope into your marriage. Ann Wilson is a delightful combination of an honest girlfriend, inspirational coach, and compassionate mom as she shares her own story of God's transformation in her heart and marriage.

DR. JULI SLATTERY, author, *Finding the Hero in Your Husband*
and *God, Sex, and Your Marriage*; president
and cofounder, Authentic Intimacy

Look, there's no one else like Dave and Ann Wilson. They are fun, vulnerable, bracingly honest, and even hilarious. But mostly, they are deeply insightful. Read this, share it, talk about it. This is going to help a lot of women . . . and their husbands.

BRANT HANSEN, radio host; bestselling author,
Unoffendable and *The Men We Need*

Whenever I spend time with my friends Ann and Dave, I hear two things—honesty and joy. And this book with encouragement from Ann and reflections from Dave has plenty of both. Wise and timely, and well worth reading.

DANE ORTLUND, senior pastor, Naperville Presbyterian Church;
author, *Gentle and Lowly*

HOW TO
SPEAK LIFE
TO YOUR
HUSBAND

HOW TO SPEAK LIFE TO YOUR HUSBAND

WHEN ALL YOU WANT TO DO IS YELL AT HIM

ANN WILSON

WITH JOHN DRIVER

WITH REFLECTIONS BY DAVE WILSON

ZONDERVAN
BOOKS

ZONDERVAN BOOKS

How to Speak Life to Your Husband
Copyright © 2025 by Dave and Ann Wilson

Published in Grand Rapids, Michigan, by Zondervan. Zondervan is a registered trademark of The Zondervan Corporation, L.L.C., a wholly owned subsidiary of HarperCollins Christian Publishing, Inc.

Requests for information should be addressed to customercare@harpercollins.com.

Zondervan titles may be purchased in bulk for educational, business, fundraising, or sales promotional use. For information, please email SpecialMarkets@Zondervan.com.

ISBN 978-0-310-36902-8 (audio)

Library of Congress Cataloging-in-Publication Data

Names: Wilson, Ann, 1960- author. | Wilson, Dave, 1957 October 15- author.
Title: How to speak life to your husband : when all you want to do is yell at him / Ann Wilson with reflections by Dave Wilson.
Description: Grand Rapids, Michigan : Zondervan Books, [2025]
Identifiers: LCCN 2024054332 (print) | LCCN 2024054333 (ebook) | ISBN 9780310368991 (trade paperback) | ISBN 9780310369004 (ebook)
Subjects: LCSH: Marriage—Religious aspects—Christianity. | Husbands—Religious life. | Man-woman relationships—Religious aspects—Christianity. | BISAC: RELIGION / Christian Living / Love & Marriage | RELIGION / Christian Living / Family & Relationships
Classification: LCC BV835 .W56474 2025(print) | LCC BV835 (ebook) | DDC 248.8/44—dc23/eng/20250109
LC record available at https://lccn.loc.gov/2024054332
LC ebook record available at https://lccn.loc.gov/2024054333

Unless otherwise noted, Scripture quotations are taken from the Holy Bible, New International Version®, NIV®. Copyright © 1973, 1978, 1984, 2011 by Biblica, Inc.® Used by permission of Zondervan. All rights reserved worldwide. www.Zondervan.com. The "NIV" and "New International Version" are trademarks registered in the United States Patent and Trademark Office by Biblica, Inc.® • Scripture quotations marked AMP are taken from the Amplified® Bible (AMP). Copyright © 2015 by The Lockman Foundation. Used by permission. www.lockman.org. • Scripture quotations marked ESV are taken from the ESV® Bible (The Holy Bible, English Standard Version®). Copyright © 2001 by Crossway, a publishing ministry of Good News Publishers. Used by permission. All rights reserved. • Scripture quotations marked NLT are taken from the Holy Bible, New Living Translation. Copyright © 1996, 2004, 2015 by Tyndale House Foundation. Used by permission of Tyndale House Publishers, Inc., Carol Stream, Illinois 60188. All rights reserved. • Scripture quotations marked PHILLIPS are taken from The New Testament in Modern English by J. B. Phillips. Copyright © 1960, 1972 J. B. Phillips. Administered by the Archbishops' Council of the Church of England. Used by permission.

Any internet addresses (websites, blogs, etc.) and telephone numbers in this book are offered as a resource. They are not intended in any way to be or imply an endorsement by Zondervan, nor does Zondervan vouch for the content of these sites and numbers for the life of this book.

This book is intended for informational and educational purposes only and does not constitute professional advice. Readers should consult licensed professionals, such as therapists or counselors, for personalized guidance and support. The author and publisher disclaim any liability for actions taken based on the information provided in this book.

Published in association with the literary agency of Wolgemuth & Wilson.

Cover design: Studio Gearbox
Cover illustration: Shutterstock
Interior design: Kait Lamphere

Printed in the United States of America
25 26 27 28 29 LBC 5 4 3 2 1

CONTENTS

INTRODUCTION

———

If you're reading this book, I'm guessing you've always wanted a great marriage. Me too! I not only wanted it; I chased it. Anticipated it. And yes, I will admit I had lofty expectations for it. I harbored certain ideas about what I would be like as a wife (hopefully amazing) and what Dave would be like as a husband (spectacular in every way). I could see it. Taste it. I knew it. We would be great together because our love would conquer all. And our great God would bless us.

Perhaps you've had your own similar dreams and expectations. But then things didn't go quite the way you expected.

So what happened?

We took off the rose-colored glasses and started to really see our spouses. And when we got honest, we had to admit this whole marriage thing was way harder than we anticipated—mainly because we both had to get to know a whole other person, with all their quirks and personality traits. And yep, I'm just going to say it: my husband is *way* different than I thought he would be. In fact, it only took about six months to feel like we had made a big mistake. We didn't know how to resolve conflict. We had different ideas about what a healthy sex life should look like. All told, each of us was often disappointed in the other, which made us pull away from each other.

It didn't take many days of matrimony for everything to legitimately become all his fault: The messy house. The crazy schedule. Even my bad moods. Everything.

Yes, it took time to reach this state of mind. There was a honeymoon phase that lasted through the first year or so, but once we had settled into early patterns of marriage, I pretty quickly came to believe that if only Dave just got his act together, we could be truly great. But that wasn't happening because he *wasn't* changing; instead, *I* was changing, becoming a person I barely recognized anymore—someone who was displeased, critical, and argumentative. Yet everything I *was* doing felt justified by everything Dave *wasn't* doing.

Have you ever been there?

The truth is, *nothing* has changed me more than my relationship with Dave. Nothing has made me rely on God more than living this life with Dave. Nothing has helped me to see the brokenness of my own soul (in a good way) more than my marriage. Marriage is funny like that. It can bring out the very best in us, but it can also bring out the very worst. I had heard such platitudes before getting married, but I never thought they would be true of me—that is, of my marriage. Until one day, they were.

It has been hard, but over the course of a few critical years in our marriage, I found hope and help—and you can too.

I've had the privilege of rubbing shoulders with and mentoring thousands of incredible women over the years. I have identified with their struggles, joys, and heartaches in the highs and lows of marriage. This is why one of my greatest passions is to help women avoid the many mistakes I made and discover how powerful and influential God has created them to be.

Yes, this is the key truth you're about to hear many times and in many different ways in the pages to come: *God has put within you the ability to bring out the best in those around you, including your husband.* Most women don't realize the power and influence they carry within them, or why it's there. This is not about being a doormat or not holding our husbands responsible for their shortcomings. We will explore all of that in detail, but for now, I invite you to give these ideas a chance to breathe and to be willing to explore them in an intentional way.

Here's the tricky part. We can use our power to bring life, hope, and wholeness to our marriages, or we can use it to bring division, devastation, and death. The path to deciphering the differences is not for the faint of heart. But girl, you got this! And trust me, it is so worth it. Let's do this together.

To begin, let me take you back to the day it all started.

CHAPTER 1

ALL HE HEARD WAS "BOO!"

Death and life are in the power of the tongue.

PROVERBS 18:21 ESV

I love hanging out with and speaking to women. So when the Mothers of Preschoolers group (MOPS) at the church Dave and I helped found in Troy, Michigan, graciously invited me to speak at one of their weekly gatherings, I said yes. Normally, it would not have been a daunting task. But that particular week, my internal wife-and-mom tank was running too close to empty. If there had been a warning light, it would have been blinking furiously for the previous ten days or so. At that time, our three small boys—C. J., Austin, and Cody—were all under the age of eight. To say our lives were hectic, crazy, and out of control would be an understatement.

It didn't help that Dave was rarely home. Not only was he a co-leading pastor at our church, but he was also the Detroit Lions NFL team chaplain, which meant he attended every home and away game. He also played softball and basketball in a men's league a couple nights a week, and he often led Bible studies in the evenings, including preaching at the Wednesday night midweek service at church. He was undeniably busy.

Even so, I was harboring feelings of abandonment and resentment toward him because I was the one staying home to raise our three energetic boys. I felt isolated, unsupported, and alone. These were valid emotions. As we will explore, the right response does not require the invalidation of our feelings or the actual facts of a difficult situation. In other words, when it came to helping me out with our crazy family, it was true that Dave was dropping a lot of balls, though I knew he wasn't doing it intentionally. And I wasn't wrong for pointing out that fact. But at that moment, I felt like I was treading water all alone in an endless sea of little boys' snot, tears, mud, and poop! Too gross? Sorry. I digress into "boy world."

The invitation from these precious women to speak at their group was an honor, but in my state of crisis, I had no clue what I should talk about. Furthermore, as a mom living in complete bedlam, teaching other moms about *anything* seemed like a stretch. After all, I was already stretched to my breaking point. What could I possibly share with them that wouldn't be phony or fake?

Then it hit me. *Ask Dave!*

Yes, I was dealing with difficult emotions about him, but this was one of those times he could actually jump in and offer the exact help I needed. Speaking to groups of people was literally his day job. In fact, doing something like this together might even help me feel like we were on the same team, accomplishing a common goal—together.

When I floated the idea past Dave, I told him that a man's perspective would be exactly what would make the whole event really shine. Dave ecstatically agreed, and just like that, the table was set for a glorious, low-stress, collaborative experience curated by two spouses on the same page with each other. I was so relieved.

When the day of the talk finally arrived, it was instantly apparent I had made the right decision to ask Dave to share. This guy came in hot with strong energy, enthusiasm, and eloquence. "Ladies," he charmingly began, "I want you to know what it's like to be a man. You see, most little boys have moms who spend each day cheering for them. 'Good job, David! Good job, Billy!' Little boys crave this kind of praise. That's why they eventually invite it. 'Mom, watch this!' They can always expect their mothers to respond with, 'Way to go! Good job!'"

Dave was really onto something here. I leaned in with the rest of the women, riveted by his quality storytelling and insight into the male psyche on the topic of affirmation, as he went on. "This continues as we get older. I played sports all the way through school, and I could still always count on certain teachers or coaches paying attention when I got an A on a test or scored a touchdown. They always said, 'Yes! Good job! You're the man!'"

This was stuff I had never heard before. I was mesmerized by his stories, amazed at how compelling he was. Dave continued with the same narrative—all the way through his college years of being the star quarterback and hearing a stadium full of people cheering him on.

Then things began to get more personal, and I liked it . . . at first. "Then I met Ann, and we just seemed to click. We wanted the same things in life and family, so we started dating. The same thing probably happened to you and your spouse. Throughout the dating years, we men hear the same message we've always heard: 'Out of all the men in the universe, I CHOOSE YOU!' You're so proud of us. It is as if you're applauding us: 'You're not only *the man*; you're *the only man* I want for the rest of my life.'" He was so animated at this point that we were all on the edge of our seats. He clapped his hands and started cheering, just to drive home his point.

I beamed with pride. *Yes*, I thought, *now this is the strong, accomplished, brilliant, sexy man I have indeed chosen. I made a good choice.* (If there was some way to insert an audible record scratch into a written sentence, I would do it here.)

"And then," Dave said as he let out a deep, breathy, depressive sigh, "we got married." As quickly as he had taken in all the energy in the room, he became sullen and crestfallen, speaking in a deadpan voice. The women shifted uncomfortably in their chairs as a few awkward giggles spilled out. I could feel side-eyed glances in my direction, scanning my face to see how I would respond to the sudden change in Dave's demeanor once, you know, his marriage to me was mentioned. I stared forward, not wanting my face to show the fear I was feeling about where he might be going with this.

Then came the final blow. He began to speak more softly, more slowly: "We men walk through the door at the end of a hard day . . ." He paused for effect, just before his words became louder, crisper, and more carefully enunciated, "and all we hear is, 'Boo! Boo!'" The more he booed, the more he seemed to regain the energy he had put aside when he started talking about our marriage. He got louder and louder, eventually cupping his hands and looking directly at me as he yelled, "Boo!"

That's when his eyes met mine. Whatever crazy Mr. Hyde break with reality he was having suddenly became apparent to his more sensible inner Dr. Jekyll. I think my eyes said it all. *What are you doing? What are you saying? And where are you going to sleep tonight?*

He seemed to awaken from his temporary trance, knowing there was no going back. What was said was said. Some of the back-and-forth that followed is fuzzy, but I think we had a small passive-aggressive exchange right there in front of all the women, which made things even more awkward. To be totally honest, I'm not sure how our talk actually ended. Somehow we made it out to the parking lot, walking together in ice-cold silence.

As soon as we were in the privacy of our own car, it was on. My embarrassment was long gone, and anger surfaced in its place, pouring out of every fiber of my being. "Are you kidding me, Dave! What the heck happened back there?"

His face turned red, and he turned away from me. I couldn't tell if he was mad or embarrassed. "I guess we've never really talked about that before, have we?"

"About me incessantly booing you? Uh, no, Dave, we have not!" He could probably feel the daggers darting from my eyes as I ranted on. "Is that really how you feel about me?"

Dave took a deep breath. "You know, I guess so. It just

feels like I can never be good enough. You have to fix or tweak everything I do. Ann, honestly it feels like you're never happy or satisfied with anything I do."

I'm glad this book is for women because I don't have to dance around the emotions that welled up inside me at that moment. In my honest estimation, I was doing the lioness's share of the daily tasks for our family—cooking, cleaning, hostage negotiations among the boys when their daily disagreements escalated. I was also working a part-time job. I was the first one up at the crack of dawn, and I was often the last one to collapse into bed like a sack of dirt. I was not doing all this for any recognition, but I certainly felt it was unfair to be criticized by the other supposed adult (right or wrong, that's how I felt at the time) in our house for not being "cheery" enough for him when he finally walked in the door after being gone all day to a thousand other enchanted places and adventures he was actively choosing over pitching in with his own family.

"Are you kidding me?" I yelled back. "Dave, I'm not booing you; I'm *helping* you!"

Before the words had barely left my lips, he shot back in a morose tone, "Well, it doesn't feel like help." Then he begrudgingly added, "Do you think it's working?"

He had finally asked the right question.

"No!" I replied loudly. "It's obviously not working, which is why I have to say it louder and more often, because it's not working at all."

I stopped in my tracks, wide-eyed with shock at what I had just admitted.

Dave continued. "It feels like you're just booing my every move, or my lack of moving, or even my ideas about moving.

It just feels like I'm only ever reminded of the things I do wrong. You constantly critique me. Heck, sometimes I even get critiqued in comparison to other husbands." He was getting worked up again, revealing that his feelings were not a temporary anomaly he had tailor-made for his presentation.

I was speechless.

Then he dropped the final bomb: "Who wants to come home to that?"[1]

MINEFIELDS

If you're a woman reading this, there's a good chance your internal antennae of concern have already involuntarily gone up about this story—and perhaps will go up about the chapters to follow. You may be worried this book is going to tell overworked and mistreated women to acquiesce or pander to the men in their lives, simply because "being nice" is what they should do (or, worse yet, what God requires them to do), while the men get to do whatever they want without any heavenly or earthly expectations or consequences. Or you might be wondering whether this book is going to fall in line with a culture that is sometimes guilty of teaching women to senselessly bash men and traditional values and to demand special treatment simply because of their gender.

I can assure you this book is not going to do any of that.

The age we live in is a veritable minefield of troubles and offenses when it comes to talking about the roles of women and men in relationships—much of which is for very good reason. Over the course of time and history, there is no doubt that women have often been—and sometimes still continue to be—overlooked, controlled, and mistreated by men, organizations, and systems. There is no excuse for such things nor is there any sound biblical or theological justification.

As these pages will reveal, God intends so much better for his daughters, regardless of the abuse and misogyny many women have faced—sometimes from religious structures or even directly in the name of Jesus. For these reasons, let me identify and unearth some of the mines that could otherwise hurt us before we take more steps across the field ahead of us.

First of all, the principles and concepts in this book are intended to be processed and applied to relationships and marriages that are not facing longstanding or imminent crises of emotional or physical abuse. If you are in such a situation, with tears in my eyes, I am praying for you and encourage you to keep trying to find the opportunity to reach out to the proper authorities or resources for help. I pray you find safety and healing as quickly as possible. If you are in danger, the principles of this book are not what you need to focus on in these moments. Getting safe and healthy should be your highest priority.

Apart from these kinds of crises, we still have plenty of other mines to avoid. Much of this book will deal with the ways we women tend to process and justify our communication patterns. But because this conversation is so fraught, it's all too easy to become fixated on what I, the author, am *not* saying instead of what I *am* saying. Everything I offer here is meant to help you love your spouse better and communicate more effectively. Please read on with this vision as your lens.

Yes, the world may be broken and people may be messy,

making marriage hard (or harder than it needs to be), but God's grace still shines in the darkness, reaching out to each of us and granting us steady guidance in the midst of this chaotic world. Which means that any despising or booing the very people we've been put here to love is counterintuitive to God's ways that reflect his grace—and makes life kind of a bummer instead of a gift. But no matter how difficult or negative things may be at the moment, the marriage you have right now in this time and place is a divine gift that is intended to be life-giving for you and your spouse.

Yet even though our marriages are a gift, we need to acknowledge that social media, politics, and our now common ways of interacting with people make it easy to seek and find only the extremes, leaving behind the work that lies in the messy middle. Making definitive judgments or conclusions is easier and faster than sitting in tension and nuance. Attacking or defending tribes is easier than listening intently to what a person is actually saying, regardless of their tribe.

Why all these buildups and disclaimers? If you're honest with yourself, you already know why. If I were to tell you that this book is just about how women communicate, specifically to the men in their lives, the tribal extremes would start a bonfire and burn us out of these pages before we even started.

Those on one side may immediately conclude—before I've really said anything of substance, by the way—that this is yet another antiquated and religious resource attempting to brainwash or disempower women, convincing them that men are not responsible for their actions and that women should always submit, even when the person they are submitting to is acting in ways that are childish, irresponsible, or aggressive.

Conversely, those on the other side may instantly assume (also without first reading the words written after this chapter because they've decided they already know what I'll say) that this book is just the breath of traditional, family-value-blown air that this crazy world of liberals really needs right now—a return to the good old days when women were quite content to be unquestioningly subservient to their men, being sure not to rock the boat by bringing up their own emotions, needs, or complaints. After all, boys will be boys, and they shouldn't really be held responsible for their mischief, even as men.

Though these two extremes blare differing conclusions, they adopt an identical approach—they make men and women and their relationships with each other simple to a fault (well, specifically, to *someone else's* fault). The real, messy, yet accessible center of any sound mutually growing relationship—which is where God's Word directs us to go—is a place where neither party declares themselves or their spouse to be a winner or loser. Here, there is no hero or villain. Instead, each of us acknowledges our equal need for grace, along with our equal divine call to offer it to each other.

Think about it. If Romans 3:23 is really true—that "all have sinned and fall short of the glory of God"—then we should always take note when we fancy ourselves or our perspectives to be absolutely correct. If women are always the heroes, Romans 3:23 is no longer true. Conversely, if men are always the heroes, the same rings true. Yes, our "opponent" may be in error, but they are not the only one capable of falling short of any standard. Harboring such mutual humility ends the constant search for conclusive heroes and villains. It makes us more compassionate and forgiving, which makes any marriage better. And really, I have found that there is only one true, ultimate hero of not only my life but also my marriage. Jesus won't fail you, and he can always be trusted.

Please also pay close attention to what I'm *not* saying—because it's all too easy to make inferences. I'm not saying that men don't make boneheaded mistakes; they can and do. I'm not saying they shouldn't be held responsible for their words or actions; they should. I'm not saying that women should not stand up or speak up for themselves; they should.

The truth is that what I hope to communicate in the following chapters aligns with neither of the extremes mentioned above nor any other extremes. It is my goal that this book will not disempower you as a woman. On the contrary, I want to see you empowered in ways you never thought possible. Words like *empower* and *disempower* have been hijacked at all kinds of points along the political and ideological spectrum, but the kind of empowerment I'm referring to is not merely theoretical or pseudospiritual. It is, instead, real, practical, and potent. It does not excuse the actions or words of anyone around us. It does not cause one to be unhealthily controlled or lost in a relationship. Rather, it will help you to exercise self-control and divinely empowered influence in healthy, lasting ways.

This journey of empowerment redeems the very term itself, returning us to the safety of God's best intentions that cannot be contained by either extreme—hypermasculine Christianity or hyperfeminine progressivism. It is not transactional in nature, meaning I won't be teaching you how to fake a smile to get what you want out of your man.

This path is gentle but rebellious. It is hard in a soft way. It leads us not only to *speaking* truth but also to *hearing* it.

Instead of life in the minefields, it leads us to receive one of the most powerful gifts we've inherited from the divine nature of our Creator—encouragement.

CHEERERS AND MIRRORS

To be honest, I'm not even sure how we ended our talk to the moms of preschoolers that day. We have doing speaking engagements together for forty-five years, and that day onstage remains the ultimate low of all our experiences, so much so that I thought I would never tell a soul about it. I was mad, and I mean the hot kind of mad! I would love to say that everything blew over in a couple hours, but a hurricane had a better chance of doing that. However, after Dave and I talked in the car, the storm became more internal. I started asking myself, *Could Dave be telling the truth? Am I always booing him?*

I just couldn't find a clear answer, mainly because it all seemed to be a simple matter of practicality and justice. I was doing more, seemingly caring more, and certainly carrying more of our family's mental and physical load than Dave was. It didn't feel fair or just. Dave was a good man—I never doubted that. But he needed some serious help remembering what he was supposed to do to keep afloat this whole teetering thing we call marriage and family. He needed me to speak the truth to him. He needed me to help him improve as a man because, as I saw it, there was no other hope of him becoming the man I thought I had married—the man I thought he should be. If someone had asked me if I could love Dave just the way he was, I think I would have answered with Max Lucado's quote about God: "God loves you just the way you are, but he refuses to leave you that way. He wants you to be just like Jesus."[2]

I thought this was part of my job—to make Dave more like Jesus. So I tried, but it wasn't working. That's because it was an assignment never given to me. It was God's job, not mine.

The truth is that I depended on Dave, which meant I wanted him to become more of the man I thought I needed. Someone had to help make that happen. I lived with him, knew him, and saw things others would never see. I could make him better, not only for me and our kids but also for the world. Plus, everyone else was always telling him how great he was. I figured his head was probably already too big. He didn't need me to build up his ego anymore.

But after several days of wrestling with myself, I thought, *Does that sound right? Like, do I really think I can make him better by critiquing and nagging him?* But I wasn't yet ready to lean all the way in to the question. After several more days of this wrestling match with my logical self, my justice-centered self, and my guilt-driven self, I stopped the fight long enough to again ask myself the question, but this time without all of the self-defensiveness: *Do I really boo Dave?*

The tricky side of sharing this part of the story is that I'm asking you to look far down the road to where we're going, even though I haven't yet told you how we're going to get there. Don't worry about that. There will be a lot of ground to cover, but it will be helpful to begin with the end in mind.

Things began to change for me when I finally stopped wrestling with myself and invited God to join me. I began defending myself to him. I laid out all of my complaints and my fears:

I feel so overwhelmed and underhelped. I don't feel heard or seen by Dave. I feel so lonely at times. I get everything done around here for everyone, including Dave. This just isn't fair. I shouldn't have to ask myself if I've been booing him because there are a thousand other things wrong with what he's doing.

Contrary to what many people think about prayer, just spilling it—whatever *it* may be—is the best kind of prayer. God loves it when we dialogue with him and confess—that is, tell the truth about—our circumstances to him. As we will learn later on in the book, King David was quite the complainer, but when he took his complaints to God, we got the book of Psalms. God is not afraid of, nor is he limited by, our weaknesses. He does not wring his hands when we let him know how we really feel down in those super-deep, dark, and disturbing places. He does not pull away; he leans in.

After I had finally laid it all out before him, I felt my inner self become more still. I sat in silence, feeling spent and unsure of what to do. That's when I felt God lean in and whisper, *Cheer for him.*

What? Wait a minute, I couldn't have heard that correctly because it almost sounded like you said, "Cheer for Dave."

After a few minutes had passed, it became apparent that I had heard the Lord accurately. I didn't like it, but I began to open my heart to what he was suggesting.

The yearslong process that followed (and that I'm still figuring out today) is reflected in the book you now hold in your hands. I didn't change in an instant. That's not how life works. You can't change something until you realize it needs to be changed. A wall will not repaint itself a different color. Someone has to evaluate the wall, buy the supplies, and take brushes and rollers to its surface. They have to want it painted a different color—and then they have to take the time to paint it.

It was clearly time for me to stop looking only at Dave and start taking a look in the mirror. Ah, there's the rub. So let me remind you again: This did not mean that Dave (or your significant other) didn't need to do the same for himself. It just means that his problems did not negate the fact that I had problems of my own as well. The long and short of it is that my long list of Dave's perceived or actual wrongs did not justify my perceived list of shorter, more "innocent" wrongs.

My granddaughter likes Taylor Swift. In her song "Anti-Hero," Taylor sings one short line that pertains to all of this: "I'll stare directly at the sun, but never in the mirror." Even if you aren't a Swifty, maybe these words will hit you. Scripture shares a similar thought:

> "And why worry about a speck in your friend's eye when you have a log in your own? How can you think of saying to your friend, 'Let me help you get rid of that speck in your eye,' when you can't see past the log in your own eye? Hypocrite! First get rid of the log in your own eye; then you will see well enough to deal with the speck in your friend's eye." (Matthew 7:3–5 NLT)

Having a log in your eye is a pretty big deal—I don't recommend it. But not *realizing* you have a log in your eye is another level of self-delusion.

When I stopped staring only at the glaring issues in my husband, I was able not only to see my own previously self-justified faults in our relationship, but also to accept God's help in making a monumental change. It quite honestly produced within me a shocking superpower hidden all along in the plain sight of Scripture.

I promise there isn't a simple, catchall fix to all of your marriage problems. In fact, if someone tries to tell you there is, you will probably find that a sales pitch will quickly follow. Don't buy it. Real people in real relationships have real problems. This means our husbands have real problems.

I wanted more out of Dave. For example, I wanted us to have more frequent family devotions, and I wanted Dave to lead them—he was, after all, a pastor. I wanted him to care about my life and how I was doing. I wanted him to see me, hear me, and actually be interested in my dreams, frustrations, and desires. I also wanted him to be invested in our kids—emotionally and spiritually—and maybe rub my feet every now and again! (Okay, that last one was a bit on the dreamy side of things.)

Despite Dave's deficiencies, God's gentle encouragement gave me the peace and courage to begin to hear what Dave was saying about me. I began to contemplate for the first time what it must be like for him to be married to me. No matter what I was saying to him or how valid the issues were, there was something I was doing that made it all come out like criticism. Dave could only hear me booing. But this led to a difficult question: How was I to change what I was doing when I still saw things that needed to be changed in him? It was going to take a change of heart.

Here's another important question to ask: Would you want

your son to be married to someone like you? Don't just blow by this question. Take a moment to really think it through. In other words, what is it like to be married to you? Is your husband excited to walk into your home because your words bring him life? I began to wonder if Dave was spending so much of his life away from our home, at least in some part, because he felt cheered out there and booed by me. In talking this through with God, I realized he had given me the power to change that—not just with my husband, but with my sons as well.

When I stopped looking into the sun and took a glance in the mirror instead, I realized I had been crushing Dave's spirit in our own home. And Dave wasn't the only casualty. My boys were also taking friendly fire from me. I was the one in their lives who always pointed out that their attitudes were stinky and that they played too many video games. Of course, these things were true, but how I communicated the truth was leading them away from a higher truth of their safety, love, and acceptance in our home, regardless of their performance.

Proverbs 21:9 doesn't pull any punches: "Better to live on a corner of the roof than share a house with a quarrelsome wife." Nice, Solomon . . . real nice. It's a cringy verse, one that women understandably shy away from reading or posting on their social media feeds. But there is much to learn from this verse, not the least being that it was originally written in ancient Hebrew and then translated into English, a language that did not even exist when it was first composed. We are now viewing it through the lens of a modern culture in which the treatment of women has rightly become a matter of more urgent concern. These and many other important factors notwithstanding, I decided I needed to pay attention to the heart of the verse.

We were enduring a classically cold Michigan winter at the time, and so I imagined Dave hanging out on the corner of our roof in the frigid air. He had a cute little beanie on his bald head and mittens that weren't going to keep his fingers warm enough in such glacial conditions. My imaginary self called out to him from the open front door, "Honey, do you want to come inside? It's freezing out there." Behind me, inside our house, was a crackling fire, hot chocolate, a comfy bed, and everything else he would need to feel safe and warm at home with the one he loved most.

Upon hearing my voice, Imaginary Dave's eyes became wide as he searched for a good excuse. "Uh, no thank you, babe. I'm doing great up here." He began to blow into his cold, cupped hands. "Maybe just toss me up a pillow and the down comforter from the bed."

Putting all of Solomon's valid and well-documented issues with women aside, this verse bears a truth equally applicable to *both* genders—*no one* responds well to being constantly hounded, chided, or drawn into a quarrel, *even* if they are often in the wrong. So, yes, if a woman had written this passage, the principle would still have rung equally true for men. When anyone is constantly badgered or rarely encouraged, the cold shingles of the roof start looking better and better with each biting remark. To put it plainly, the person on the roof feels booed.

And then it hit me: I had been booing Dave for a long time. No wonder he was spending more time outside our home than inside it.

And in that moment of recognition, my journey toward becoming an encourager began—first with an honest look at my own life and then followed by a decision to obey what God was telling me to do. I began learning how to cheer more than boo—and to do it in a way that wasn't fake or inauthentic. Yes, Dave and I still have arguments. Yes, Dave is still sometimes wrong. Yes, there are times when I have to speak difficult truths to him. However, as we'll see, I began to embrace one of the unique superpowers God offers—empowering others through encouragement.

THE POWER OF EMPOWERMENT

Now that you see where I was, I can warn you that the journey ahead is not for the faint of heart. However, if you're a wife, mother, or single woman already navigating this crazy world, I'm not worried about your ability to make it. Your unique life is a gift from a Father who infuses his daughters with strength, purpose, and meaning—all traits reflective of his image. As you start on this journey of empowerment, you'll see the positive power you can wield and how to use it for good. I certainly did.

I know what you're wondering: *Did all of Ann's cheering lead to better behavior from Dave?* Actually, it did. But seeking behavioral change in others shouldn't be the goal. If it is, it will only become a recipe for shallowness, manipulation, and disappointment. Instead, this journey is about truly becoming the woman God intended you to be all along, endowed with power, wisdom, and influence that surpass all the counterfeit definitions bombarding us in this dark world.

Grace-based marriage looks very different from what our

culture deems as normal. It is a relationship in which both spouses acknowledge their respective faults and, more importantly, also acknowledge a common need for the same grace from the same healer. When we take our eyes solely off of our spouse and look at ourselves as well, we will realize just how much we need the same amazing grace we are so often unwilling to give to our spouse.

My hope and prayer is that we can learn together how to demonstrate true humility toward people, a humility that does not remove our value or voice. I want to help you *find* your voice, not lose it. I want to sit with you and explore the power of the tongue in ways that go far beyond mere positive confessions, diving instead into the scriptural invitations that beckon us to practice honest affirmation as an act of powerful, rebellious grace. And I want to show you why real grace is so rebellious. I will help you understand why men often show up in a better way outside the home than when they come home to their families, and how this may not be right or acceptable—and how responding in the wrong way will certainly never make it so.

It's time to stop booing your man. In the following chapters, I'll show you how.

DAVE'S REFLECTION

Hi, I'm Dave.

It may feel like we've already met. I'm the guy who didn't realize he was loudly booing his wife in the middle of a presentation. Not my proudest moment, but it was one of my most honest moments.

Ann has asked me to pop in and add some reflections throughout the book to what she and you have been discussing. Sounds a bit familiar, doesn't it—Ann inviting me along to something she is speaking about? Look, I promise you I won't start booing. On the contrary, I actually want to do the opposite. I want to cheer on my wife (and you) by helping you see how everything she is sharing has transformed our marriage and, by God's grace, my life. That's how he often works. He uses our relationships with other people, especially our spouses, as tools in his hands to chisel, shape, and craft us into someone new. Ann has been the most beautiful, patient, and willing human God has used to shape me. I am the man I am today because of her patience and belief in me. She is an amazing gift.

So I get how this looks. Sometimes in our culture (especially church culture), when a woman has the microphone, it seems a man invariably has to follow up with a recap of what she just said, perhaps in a foolish way that attempts to fill in any supposed gaps in her logic, things she might have missed that the man can "obviously" explain in a better way. Women affectionately refer to this practice as "mansplaining." And as far as I can tell, women love mansplaining.

All joking aside (just for a second), I make a solemn vow not to mansplain in these reflections. The only gaps I plan to fill are ones that Ann is too humble to express—that is, all the ways she was patient and willing to change when I didn't yet know how. I simply want to offer my perspective on how these biblical attitudes and actions have truly made a difference in our marriage, even when they arose from my many boneheaded moments and foolish mistakes. God's grace takes what appears worthless and redeems it into treasure. He can always take our difficult circumstances and make something good out of them.

It has been several decades since I told Ann that I felt like she was always booing me. Those feelings arose from the fact that I felt respected in almost every other relationship and role in my life except those of husband and father. And while I certainly have pride issues to continue to bring before God (we all do), this was not just a matter of needing endless affirmation, no matter what I had done or was doing. It was something deeper, which I didn't quite have the words to fully express. And it's why it takes *How to Speak Love to Your Husband* to unpack this concept more completely.

Over time, Ann walked a path with God that led her to decide to change her booing into cheering. She began to speak words of life—words of respect, words that didn't only state all that I was missing, but rather words that acknowledged me as a person who was valuable to her, apart from my success or failure on that particular day. I went from feeling like I was capable only of letting her down to feeling like she loved and respected me as an equal—and as a man. And let me tell you, this feeling made me want to work hard to live up to the high regard she had for me. It made me want to be the man she saw that I was capable of becoming. When you truly believe in your husband (or sons), we *feel* it. And that belief motivates us to become better men. No doubt this is just as true for women as for men, but all I know is that when Ann started celebrating who I was instead of just criticizing me, it motivated me to new levels as a husband and father.

Obviously, I was not yet the man she was telling me I was. I may never fully be. Obviously, Ann is not able to transform my life; she is pretty awesome, but she is not the Almighty. Besides, that is way too much weight for her to carry—a weight that I see many wives carry as they desperately try to transform their marriages and families into something better.

No, the wife isn't meant to carry the weight of transformation. For us—as we have always said in our talks and books—there had to be a third party involved. If we were the two parallel points on a horizontal lower plane, we needed a third, vertical point on a higher plane. When we finally were willing to listen to and lean into God's ways, his already present grace was suddenly fully aligned with our issues, forming the vertical completion and transformation of our marriage that we could never achieve on our own.

Ann is right—well, except for perhaps one thing (sorry, honey). She said that this journey ahead is *not* for the faint of heart. I know what she means, but I think it is *exactly* for the faint of heart. How do I know? I'm the guy who is often faint of heart. Maybe you are too.

Yet I've learned that God is for me and with me. And the most effective, tangible way I've learned this has been through the loving, respectful, superpowered, genuine affirmation of my wife, which she uses daily to see, strengthen, and sustain my faint heart. It has also made me more loving, respectful, and genuinely affirming of her in return. God's ways often work out that way. You give something away that you desperately want to hold on to, and, in turn, God gives you something you desperately wanted but could never attain on your own.

I watch my wife use her God-given superpower of affirmation on a daily basis, and in ways I could never even fathom for myself. It is a unique thing of wonder, beauty, and power to behold. Through it, God speaks life to countless people through her voice. I'm excited that you get to learn how God wants to accomplish the same thing through you.

But I'm most excited that when it comes to receiving Ann's life-giving superpower of encouragement, you get to be next.

CHAPTER 2

STOP THE CHOP

An excellent wife is the crown of her husband,
but she who brings shame is like rottenness in
his bones.

PROVERBS 12:4 ESV

The cold Michigan wind-whipped snow invaded my hood, chilling the back of my neck all the way down my spine. I had just stepped out of the car to hurry through a snow-drifted parking lot into the kids' school for parent-teacher conferences. I walked by myself—again. Dave had to attend a church meeting of some sort. By this point, we had two boys in middle school and one in elementary. I walked alone into their schools, my internal resentment meter creeping up to another level.

After what felt like hours of conversing with teachers and hearing their insights about our kids, I drove home and walked into the house, hoping Dave would be home. More importantly, I was hoping he would have the kids in bed. Of course, he was *not* home. Besides that, the house was a mess, with a pile of dirty dishes in the sink, and the boys were completely zombied-out, playing video games in the basement.

Ugh! Why do I have to do everything?

I broke the boys out of their video game trance, talked to them about what their teachers had said, prayed with them, and put them to bed. Afterward, I straightened up the house and tackled the mountain of dirty dishes. I did the work, but my mind was elsewhere. The entire time, I wrestled with the inner dialogue in my head:

He doesn't help.

He doesn't listen.

I carry the load.

Everything in his life is more important than our family.

An hour later, Dave got home. He probably thought he was finally going to come in from the cold, but instead he was headed straight into an indoor blizzard of cold-hearted resentment. The feelings had been swirling inside me since about the time I stepped into the snow in the school parking lot. With so much time on my hands to do, you know, the aforementioned jobs around the house that, quite frankly, Dave should have been doing, I had rehearsed all of his shortcomings and failures—and not just the ones from that evening. I was like Elsa, the Ice Queen, and I had manufactured a full-scale magical ice palace right inside my heart. And I was not about to just *let it go.* (You know you were thinking it.)

Enter Dave, stage wrong. He walked through the door and greeted me with a hug. I let him hug me in the technical sense—I may have been a diabolical ice queen, but I'm not a monster. But as his arms wrapped around me, I ensured he felt the chill radiating from my very being. Of course, Dave could feel my frostiness, but he was given to avoiding conflict, so he simply sighed and walked to the living room. He turned on the TV, trying to escape his stressful day for a few minutes with a football game. I suppose he must have thought that anything would be better than dealing with me, his frosty wife.

But in my mind, he deserved the treatment I was dishing out. *That'll show him*, I thought. The only problem was that it didn't show him what I wanted him to see.

To that end, before we dive deeper into the biblical and relational realities of why we boo our husbands, we may still need some convincing that we are actually doing it—and what the results are.

CHOPPING PLANTS

I wish I could wrap up the previous story with a nice bow—a clean resolution that led to remorseful conversation and meaningful change. Unfortunately, I can't even remember exactly what happened that night because that same scenario cycled on repeat most nights for the first fifteen to twenty years of our marriage. It certainly became much worse once we had kids, but it was always there. We loved each other, but on these fronts, we were stuck in an eternal winter.

I bet I'm not alone. Have you been there? I've spoken to women of all ages around the world about their marriages, and I've found that most of us have gone through something like this—and in many cases, we are still going through it. It may not be parent-teacher conferences or dirty dishes (though I bet these make most women's lists); instead, it may be an overarching feeling of scarcity or disappointment with our spouses due to their lack of affection, lack of discipline, lack of planning, lack of sensitivity, lack of awareness of our needs, lack of spiritual leadership, lack of interest, lack of energy. Feel free to add your own "lack" to the list.

Whether we tell them or not, they feel our disappointment, because we make sure they do. I'm not saying that's all wrong. Our feelings are valid. The answer is not that we shouldn't ever express our feelings. And no one is saying that our husbands are not lacking in many areas. Mine certainly was. Regardless, after my long and chilly reign, God brought to my attention that I was indeed booing Dave. That was a surprise in and of itself. But imagine my shock when it became apparent that God wanted me not only to recognize that I was booing my husband, but also to change the way I had been communicating for years. But you can't simply change—that's not how it works. The journey to change is a path marked by receiving the right kind of truth and doing the right kind of work, both of which will be explored on our journey ahead.

For me, the journey began by going back and revisiting the expectations I had before I was even married. To help me do this, I visualized two big, beautiful, luscious, green houseplants in two different pots that represented two different men with different traits and characteristics.

We all do this. As we enter the dating scene, we meet and evaluate different men, analyzing their gifts, strengths, character, and, hopefully, their walk with God. We look very closely at each man—each a different plant—trying to determine the depth of their root system, the health of the leaves they produce, and so forth. Finally, after searching and inspecting, we come to the delightful conclusion that this is the perfect husband—the houseplant—we want to live with forever. We basically say, "Of all the men in the world, I choose you. You are the perfect man for me." Marriage bells ring. Mortgages follow. Kids soon scamper about.

We don't realize that in the evaluation and choosing we had real and specific expectations of what this houseplant— this husband—would be. At first, this plant is as strong and hardy as we expected. But then, after we've been married to this luscious plant of a man for a while, we see something we hadn't noticed before—a brown, withered leaf. *What's this?* we ask ourselves. *I've never seen this before.*

At first, we're not sure what the problem is. I certainly didn't when I noticed changes in Dave. So we look at the plant and conclude that it has to be something internal or something from the outside that is causing damage. Perhaps it's sweltering in the heat, not getting enough water, sitting in poor soil, or not getting enough nurturing. And this causes the plant to act differently than before—less healthy, its leaves withering and turning brown. If a man withers internally or is hampered by external challenges, he stops being romantic. He stops noticing you. He doesn't like to sit and talk to you anymore or hold your hand. Previously, he may have genuinely asked you how you were doing, but now he doesn't seem to think about you. In fact, it seems like he only acts interested in talking to you right before bed when he wants to know if you want to have sex.

What happens when we find a brown leaf on a houseplant? We get our scissors and cut it off. Why? It's not because we hate the houseplant. In fact, we're cutting off the dead leaf because we love the houseplant and want it to thrive. We don't want it to be weak and dying. So we snip and prune. Done and done. But wait, maybe that's not enough. After we cut off that one brown leaf, we can see more clearly another brown leaf hiding behind it. This brown leaf shows more failure within the plant.

So we snip again. We offer sharper words to our husband—just to make him healthier, obviously. *You don't want to show up in our family and be present. It's like you give all your best energy everywhere else. When you're home, you expect me to hold everything together while you numb out on sports or video games.* But with each snip, instead of getting healthier, that plant produces more brown leaves.

At this point, it has become our task to get rid of all the bad leaves that keep popping up. No one else is going to do it. And you know what? Those small scissors just aren't cutting it anymore. Time for the hedge clippers—that will help us finally get this plant to where it needs to be. *You never help* (chop). *You don't pray* (chop). *You're selfish* (chop). *You play video games like a child* (chop). *Or golf* (chop). *Or hunt* (chop). *You don't help with the kids* (chop). *You're hardly ever home* (chop). *You don't touch me except when you want sex* (chop). *You don't lead spiritually* (chop). We may not realize it as it's happening, but with each criticism, we're lopping off so much that, eventually, the only thing left of a once full and lively plant (of a husband) is a mutilated, stumpy remnant.

We don't like that we're left with a stump, but there are no other leaves to prune and we still want to fix our plant, so we turn our attention to other houseplants for comparison. Our neighbor has a lush, healthy, strong houseplant. Contrary to the one we've been pruning, her plant is noticeably green, full, and hardy. So we point to her beautiful plant and say to our stump, "Why aren't you more like *that* plant?"

We don't even realize that with our words and comparisons, despite our husband's already existing faults, insufficiencies, and insecurities, we are the ones cutting him down to size. No, we may not have made all of his poor choices for him—again, this is not about denying his faults or not holding him responsible for his own actions. Still, with every poor choice he makes or has ever made, we're right there to remind him. I mean, who else is going to? It's not like he's going to figure it out on his own, right?[1]

Can you see how easily the whole idea of pruning and cutting is seemingly so just and justifiable? Yet there is a very real truth that coexists within our sense of justice: Every criticism, accusation, critique, and nagging word only serves to lop off more and more of the husband until, at least when he's at home with us, he's merely a wounded stump of the man God intends him to be. The reality was, though it felt super justified in the moment, I sliced and diced a once vibrant and confident man into a withdrawn, bitter, belittled one.

Here's the profound part hidden in plain sight: In my desire to equalize the uneven power dynamics of responsibility between us, I unintentionally overlooked the power I already possessed. Because his lack of interest and effort made me feel unseen, overwhelmed, and weak in the relationship, I unconsciously used a power I didn't know I had in a destructive way—and it proved to be very potent indeed. It turned out that a mere boo could render my husband defeated and bewildered.

Ironically enough, his resulting pouty and withdrawn disposition left me feeling even more frustrated with him, so I amped up the negative words. You can guess how that worked out. For years, it was a rinse-and-repeat cycle more repetitive and predictable than the loads of laundry I resented him for never doing. Remember that list of everything he lacked? He may have been *lacking*, but I had been *hacking*. I was taking a machete to his very personhood and confidence—and all that chopping left us both wondering if he could ever become the full, vibrant, healthy man we both wanted him to be.

LIFE, DEATH, AND MY WAY OF BEING

It's not easy to admit that, in at least some area of your life, you've become a machete-wielding wife. (Now there's a sentence I never thought I'd say.) I'm not saying you are, but I can unequivocally say I was. In all honesty, I truly thought I was helping Dave. I believed I was motivating him to become a better man and husband. Instead, my cutting words were bringing a type of death to his soul.

Is *death* too strong of a word? I don't think so. On a practical level, none of us want to be in an environment where we are constantly nagged, second-guessed, and made to feel we can never do anything right. If you're honest with yourself, you probably avoid those kinds of people. I know I try to. Why? Because those kinds of people suck the life out of us. And what happens when all the life is sucked out of something or someone? *Death* happens.

One of the writers of Proverbs has no qualms about using equally strong language when referring to the power of words: "The tongue has the power of life and death, and those who love it will eat its fruit" (Proverbs 18:21 NLT). Yes, positive words can have positive effects in any situation, but the journey to becoming a wife who doesn't boo her husband is much more immersive than changing just her words alone. It actually begins in a much deeper place.

So, then, what do you do with this passage about words having the power of life and death? You recognize that words don't just appear out of nowhere. When they float to the surface, if you pay attention, you will find ropes tied to them that lead downward into deep, dark wells. You can take the words at face value, or you can keep pulling up on the ropes until you see what the words are connected to. If you keep searching the deeper places, you can find the expectations, emotions, traumas, or beliefs that are tethered to the words you use. Life and death may be reflected in your words, but they originate in the deep places of your soul.

As much as you want to do a deep dive into your husband's flaws, if you're going to experience actual change in your marriage, you must be willing to first do a deep dive into your own self. I had to ask myself why I always felt the need to critique Dave and point out ways he could do things better. Yes, the first answer you may find is pretty simple: *Uh, because*

I do everything and he does nothing. I'm not negating the simple and valid reality of this answer if it's truly the case in your marriage. However, and please know I'm saying this gently, if you're in a constant state of negative thinking and speaking toward your spouse, I promise there is more to it than just his lack of help with the family or around the house. But you have to be brave enough to search deeper to find it.

I'm embarrassed to tell you my answer to why I was always critiquing Dave. In all honesty, I knew I did a lot of things better than Dave pertaining to our home, our kids, cleaning, relationship issues, and many other areas. But when I kept pulling on the rope, something much uglier came to the surface—my pride.

You may be thinking, *It's not pride if it's true.* I thought the same thing. My attitude of superiority and condescension toward Dave felt justified because I had valid reasons for feeling that way. Dave was obviously the problem—I had mounds of evidence to prove it. Case closed. But in actuality there were *two* problems, not just one. I had been stacking Dave's long list of wrongs against my much longer list of rights. However, *being right* doesn't always mean you're *in the right*. As much as it pained me to admit, Dave wasn't the only problem. I had my own wrongs to grapple with. Unfortunately, two wrongs can never make a right.

As two parties that make up a couple, we each have strengths and weaknesses to bring to the marriage. I knew that. Even so, I wanted Dave to do things the way I did them because my way was not just one of the right ways; it was *the best* right way. His way was as plainly red and white as a one-way street sign that read, *Wrong Way.* And I was so wrapped up in believing my way was right that I became angry, losing sight of Dave's value as a human and a husband—and to top it off, I was blaming him for my anger. The truth is, I felt alone and unloved, so I fixated on one of the constants in my life—the endless household tasks. Trust me, when you find yourself ready to burn your marriage to the ground over laundry and dishes, there is something more significant going on. But it will hide in the deep, dark places until you pull it to the surface.

When I let down my guarded emotions for a moment, I began to see how much I cared about things that mattered *less* than my marriage. I mean, who cares if the kids are dressed in weird outfits and people see them? The truth is, I wasn't worried about the kids, but rather about people's perception of—you guessed it—*me*. I made my problems out to be all about Dave, but this problem at least was all mine. Because the truth was that I thought people would see our kids dressed that way and think *I* was a lame mom. Dave really wasn't involved, but he was still the main target of my emotional angst. And even when Dave did help, I was never satisfied with the help he gave. Yet, in reality, who cares how the dishwasher is loaded as long as it's loaded? Sure, they may not get as clean as when *you* load it, but is it worth berating your husband over? Or who cares if he has to ask you what needs to be done because, even after ten years of marriage, he *still* doesn't know?

I know what you're thinking: *I* care!

I blamed Dave for all of our problems, but upon deeper examination, I realized I was not blameless. Hear me: I'm not making light of a list that can dominate a mom's life for more than twelve hours a day. I know the list well, so, yes, I know it matters. I'm just asking you to go deeper for a minute so there is a chance for change in a way that's different from how you've been trying to create change up to now. In the grand scheme of things—marriage and the life you will someday have with your husband after the kids have left the nest—are these things really worth badgering your husband ad nauseam to the point that he would rather be anywhere than at home?

Should he grow up and show up? Yes, he should. Will he? You are not in control of the answer to this question, even if you want to be. More on that to come.

But for now, let's take our questions one step further. Is it really worth all the complaining, not only out loud about or to your husband but also nonstop in your own head? It may feel worth it, but besides the fact that it isn't changing your husband or your situation for the better, is it making you feel more alive or at peace? Or as Proverbs suggests, are such negative words—even if they're not always being spoken—sucking the life and joy out of you?

Believe it or not, you don't have to say negative things for your disapproval to be felt by your husband. In the Arbinger Institute's *The Anatomy of Peace*, researchers discuss the power of a person's "way of being" toward others. Their studies show that people actually instinctively feel and respond to your way of being toward them even more than your behaviors and words. In other words, people can tell if your heart is at war with them or not, even if you do everything in your power to give off a different impression. I'm sure we know that our husbands detect and "respond more to how we're regarding them than they do to our particular words or actions. We can treat [them] fairly, but if our hearts are warring toward them while we're doing it, they won't think they're being treated fairly at all. In fact, they'll respond to us as if they weren't being treated fairly."[2]

Can you see why this issue is about so much more than just using affirming words or making positive confessions? This is about the condition of our hearts because, as Jesus said, "Whatever is in your heart determines what you say" (Matthew 12:34 NLT). So before we end this chapter, I want you to know what you're getting into, because it's about more than changes in speech or behavior. This is the stuff of *heart change*—and trust me, there's only One who can truly change a heart and bring about the peace in your marriage you're longing for.

PUTTING DOWN THE SHEARS AND PICKING UP THE MIRROR

Pride—yes, I could try to deny it, but it was right there inside me. However, I began to see it only when I laid down the shears and picked up the mirror. I had to take a break from examining and chopping Dave to pursue self-examination instead. Yes, I promise we'll come back to the issues our husbands have. But I also promise you that you can't hold two things of this magnitude in your hand—and, more so, in your heart—at the same time. One thing has to be laid down for another to be picked up.

God began calling me to confess and repent of my pride and arrogance, which had truly and fully seeped into my way of being toward Dave. As we discussed before, examining the content and consistency of your inner thoughts will reveal a lot about not just how you're feeling, but about how you're being. Your mind is a powerful place that needs a powerful God who can help you to "be transformed by the renewing of your mind" (Romans 12:2). The New Living Translation reads, "Let God transform you into a new person by changing the way you think." New ways of thinking are necessary for new ways of being.

Pride. Arrogance. Ugh—I hated such words being attached to me because my intent was never to harm or discourage Dave. I actually want to help him. In the next chapter, we'll talk more about the nature of a helper, but as a setup, let's recall that in Scripture, the Holy Spirit is called our Helper (John 14:16 ESV—*parakletos* in the Greek, which can also be translated "comforter, encourager, counselor, or advocate." As the following pages will reveal, it turns out that the Spirit is a much better helper than I could be. For this reason, I can and need to trust him to do the work in Dave—and in me—that I so desperately want to do myself.

I had to accept the fact that Dave loves and walks with the Spirit too, which means he can hear from God on his own without my nagging him. Then I started learning that if I have something important I need to say to Dave that might be hard for him to hear, I should go to Jesus first and ask him how to phrase it in a way that will bring life instead of death.

But before we get into all of that, we must decide if we're brave enough to hold up the mirror and ask the question, *Do I chop my husband with my words, attitudes, facial expressions, and body language—or, in general, with my way of being?* Even more, I would encourage you to begin pondering questions to ask your husband and how you think he might respond:

- Do you feel like I boo you, or do I chop you down?
- What has it been like to be married to me?

Later on, after you've put some of this into practice, you will be able to ask these questions of your husband and hopefully already have some idea of the answers. But we're not quite there yet. The truth is that right now his brutal honesty could lead you back into the chopping cycle, which we want to avoid. And in fact, he may not be ready to answer those questions honestly, because he may not want to hurt your feelings. When it is time, you consider asking him to write out his answers, just to decrease any awkwardness or offense. In Dave's case, he waited for years to tell me the truth, but when he did, it was in front of a whole room of women. I must have been too scary to confront in the privacy of our "safe" home.

As soon as you're ready to go deeper, you can be encouraged that God is ready to begin the change in you and your marriage that you've been desperately trying to force for years. Our heavenly Father loves you, sees you, and cares about you and your marriage. It extends well beyond what you can even imagine. It's true. I'm writing this with tears in my eyes as I recall God's unfathomable grace. Years ago, at that stage in my walk with God, I was beating myself up over my failures as a mom and wife. I hated who I had become. But his love and grace began reminding me that he loves me, despite my insecurities and inconsistencies, my pride and arrogance. I had a lot that needed to be worked out. I still do. But there is so much hope.

Yes, marriage is a long game, where "the days are long,

but the years are short."³ Don't become discouraged if it takes some time to get there.

✳ ✳ ✳

I have used the "chopping plants" illustration for years on stages around the world, but I will never forget what happened the first time I shared it. Dave and I were speaking at our church to couples. After the session had ended and most people had left the auditorium, I noticed an older couple sitting alone in silence. I felt the inner nudge of the Helper to go and talk with the couple. As I got closer, I could see the older gentleman softly crying, big tears streaming down his wrinkled cheeks. Their age gave some evidence that they had been married for a long time.

As I approached, the wife looked at me earnestly with pleading eyes. She spoke with quiet urgency and an obvious sense of confusion: "I don't know what's wrong. This is my husband, and he has been crying ever since you cut that plant down. He won't tell me why he's crying."

The elderly gentleman had not looked up when I approached. He was hunched over, staring at his feet as tears ran down his face and plopped onto the floor, making miniature puddles on the concrete beneath him. He lifted his head and looked straight at me with wet, faded blue eyes. He lifted a feeble left hand and pointed to the forlorn stump of the plant that was still on the stage. "That stump is me." He choked out the words, then plunged his face into his hands, and continued with a weary cry as though it had been pent-up for decades.

His wife turned to me and, in an anguished voice, said, "I had no idea I was hurting him. I thought I was helping."

It still brings tears to my eyes to recall that elderly couple. They could have easily been Dave and me, had Dave not finally told me that I was constantly booing him.

The couple walked away carrying hard truths that offered new hope for the future. But they also faced new challenges to change their well-worn patterns of communication. We encouraged them not to go it alone, but to walk with others in the way of community and therapy. Their story is not an isolated instance. Over the years, countless men have cried on my shoulder after hearing the plant illustration, saying it put into words what they have been feeling their entire married life.

I want a great marriage, and I know you do too. I am a prime example of someone who struggles with her words and her way of being. But to this day, God's Word keeps showing me his gracious and eternal way of being toward me, softening my heart and making me more like him. And ultimately he has become my anchor, my lifeline, and a light to my sometimes-dark path. Today I can more easily let go of control and anger because I'm no longer requiring things from my husband that only my Savior can give. As I practice daily letting Jesus' light illuminate the dark places within me, he does what only he can do—change me for good. He can do the same for you.

DAVE'S REFLECTION

There was so much I wasn't doing right in our marriage and family, but I can tell you that Ann is right when she talks about realizing how her booing wasn't producing the change we both wanted. You see, I really *did* want to be a better husband and father, but I was so insecure about it and weary from trying to get there that the thought of being booed made me want to run away. The problem with feeling like you want to run is that even if you're close to home, you're still far away—and certainly far away from any meaningful or positive changes. We were stuck in this cycle, and somewhere deep down inside, I knew I really did need to change.

When Ann became willing to look in the mirror, it freed me to do the same. At first, it was a lot harder than I thought it would be. There was so much insecurity within me. In fact, when Ann first began speaking words of life to me instead of speaking only words of criticism, I didn't believe her. She had never done that, so I didn't know what to do with it. I was suspicious, believing she was just trying to get me to do more chores or be home more often.

But her consistency over a long period of time made me start trusting her words and actions. She would tell me things like, "I think you're a good man." Honestly, I pushed back. I told her that even though I appreciated her kindness, I knew it wasn't true. Why? Because even though I had a pretty good reputation the public eye and tried to convince myself I was a good man, my life at home was the biggest piece of evidence that I was a fraud. But Ann wouldn't let up—she kept telling me I was a good husband and father, even when I knew I was struggling to show up in our life.

It was crazy. Even when I would do something small, like take out the trash, she would notice and thank me for doing it. Over the course of only a few months of Ann's encouragement, I began to believe (and feel) that her way of being toward me had completely changed. I know God made it happen, because once she changed, I no longer felt pressure to change in ways I never could on my own. Instead, I felt excitement from somewhere deep within—a grace from God telling me I was no longer being judged for my shortcomings. I was being loved for who I was in Christ. That led to real changes within me. Though I didn't believe I was the man Ann said I was, I began over the course of time to want to become that man. I not only started trying harder to be the husband and father Ann knew I could be, but more so I started believing I had real value as God's son—and yes, as Ann's husband. That set me free and gave me a lot of peace.

Truthfully, I'm still not the man Ann says I am, but through her selfless courage to look within herself and love me differently, I am not the man I was back when she felt the need to boo me all the time. When Ann began speaking life into me from a place of sincerity, gratitude, and love, God used it to change me in ways neither I nor Ann thought would ever be possible. I certainly don't feel chopped down anymore. Neither do I feel falsely built up like some football team losing by sixty points that is still being cheered on by the cheerleaders on the sidelines because they have to do so to keep their scholarships.

Of course, Ann has experienced a lot of growth too, which is why I'm so excited about where she will take you in the next chapter—into the intricate ways God uses each equal spouse in a marriage to help the other become who they could never be on their own.

Take my word for it. It's much less painful than getting chopped over and over again.

CHAPTER 3

WHY DON'T *I* GET A HELPER?

The words of the godly are a life-giving fountain.

PROVERBS 10:11 NLT

Growing up, I was blessed to have a mom who was an amazing wife and mother. I didn't grow up in a Jesus-centered home, but my mom was still one of the greatest servants I've ever witnessed. She was just so very nice—quite frankly, much nicer than I was.

My dad was the person she served the most. Mom definitely had a servant's heart, but her niceness in serving a man who treated her like his actual servant was a bridge too far for me. It was common in my mom's generation, and I wanted no part of it. Dad took Mom for granted, taking advantage of her kindness and letting her overwork herself while he was content to hang back and relax. Let me tell you, seeing that made me super angry.

I harbored harsh feelings toward my dad, but honestly, I think my feelings toward my mom were even worse. After all, she was allowing him to take advantage of her. When I was older, I would confront her: "Mom, stop being so nice to him. You are enabling him to be lazy."

But what I said didn't seem to matter. Though I hated it, Mom was in a pattern she accepted. Over time, I came to understand that there was more to it than mere acceptance or resignation. She said to me one day, "You know, honey, I really like doing things for your father." I heard her mouth moving, but it was like she was speaking Greek. I just didn't get it because, from my perspective, she was allowing herself to be a doormat. Why would anyone do that? Not only did I not understand it, but I also lost respect for her because of it. The roles that she and my father were playing not only seemed outdated and antiquated; they seemed demeaning to women and avoidable altogether.

My parents' story leads us right into one of the minefields that exist around any conversation related to gender roles in marriage. So for this conversation, let's lean into God's grace and use as much care and caution as possible. When we do so, I believe we can come out on the other side in better shape than when we began.

GENESIS AND JERRY MAGUIRE

Much has been written recently about the legitimate damage that certain concepts based on unhealthy systems of patriarchy and weaponized doctrine have done to women over the centuries, especially in the church. Some men have used God's words as excuses to justify the mistreatment of women in marriages and in Christian spaces. My heart goes out to these women, and I want to repeat this truth: God's ways are irreconcilable with dominance, control, pride, deception, self-serving power, manipulation, and abuse. His ways—for men and women—are clearly evident in Scripture.

In other words, no matter how many theological degrees someone has, books they have published, or number of people in their congregation, if they reject or even downplay "love, joy, peace, patience, kindness, goodness, faithfulness, gentleness, self-control" as the clear biblical foundations of all Christ-honoring thought, behavior, and leadership (Galatians 5:22–23 ESV) God's Word says that their thoughts, behaviors, or leadership are about as useful as "a noisy gong or a clanging cymbal" (1 Corinthians 13:1 ESV). If anyone's theology or system attempts to overrule these foundational truths, even under the guise of convincing biblical study or impressive quantifiable results in ministry, they are, at best, misguided. At worst, they are misaligned with the truths of Scripture and the working of the Spirit—after all, the previous list contains the fruit of the Spirit. If this fruit is not present, beware of the claim that the Spirit is.

I say all that in order to bring clarity to the next part of our discussion because we are about to go to a place in Scripture that has often been mishandled, which can lead to dominance over women. And it has often been done by using the creation story in Genesis as its justification.

In the beginning of our marriage, Dave and I created many unhealthy patterns, unaware that they originated from somewhere else. They were shaped by our previous experiences, our unique internal wiring, and certain ways of thinking we didn't even know were bouncing around in our young newlywed heads.

The boo story revealed more than just the fact that I had been booing Dave for years. It also revealed one of these ways of thinking. I genuinely thought I was helping Dave see his problems and become a better person. So I was shocked to find that he interpreted my efforts to be quite unhelpful.

But the theme of "helper" wasn't new—and if you've grown up in certain religious circles, you probably understand why. The term is consistently used to refer to women's roles in marriage. Most of us know that the Bible reads, "In the beginning God created the heavens and the earth" (Genesis 1:1). Honestly, things get pretty complicated from there.

It takes less than two chapters for the concept of relational roles between men and women to find an expression that still produces controversy today. Genesis 2:18 seems to be where many interpretations collide, producing all kinds of sparks. "Then the LORD God said, 'It is not good that the man should be alone. I will make him a helper suitable for him.'" There's that word, the one I thought I was, and the one many still think women are created to be: woman = man's *helper*. You'll have to forgive me as I honestly mean no disrespect to God's holy Word, which I fully believe in and try to follow. But yikes! Such language makes me think of "Santa's little helper"—not exactly a term that elicits images of strength or the dignity reflective of someone fully and equally made in the image of the Creator.

When Dave and I were first married, this verse was constantly used in our church experiences as a reference to gender roles in marriage—and the general interpretation was that it meant women were not made for the important things men were made for. At least that's how my young ears heard it. I internalized the idea that women are meant to accentuate and enhance a man's desires, dreams, and—in some unhealthy circles—every whim. Genesis 2:18 was used as justification for forbidding women be in leadership positions outside their home, develop their gifts, or pursue any kind of career apart from raising children. After all, women need to be available to *help men*.

I have always loved God's Word, but I struggled with this verse. I wanted to be more than just a little helper. I wanted to change the world for Jesus and take territory for God's kingdom. I wanted to bring as many people as possible into a relationship with Christ. To be told that I could only be a little helper made me feel as if I were wearing handcuffs. Would I ever be able to see the fire blazing inside of me for God become a real ministry? I was a young wife and mother working my fingers to the bone while watching my husband pursue whatever he wanted, oblivious to how he was neglecting being an equal partner in raising our family. I was fixated on the injustice of it all. *So the husband gets a helper?* I would think very loudly in my head. *Where's* my *helper?*

It seemed to be a valid question—and honestly, it still is. I even went to the trusty old dictionary for relief. Perhaps I was thinking about this all wrong. Here's what I found: *helper* = "one that helps, a relatively unskilled worker who assists a skilled worker usually by means of manual labor." Again, yikes!

About ten years into our marriage, FamilyLife asked us to begin speaking at their Weekend to Remember marriage conferences. I was twenty-nine years old at the time. This was a huge honor, and although I was young, I didn't want to miss a great opportunity to help couples. However, I figured I would be expected to toe the line on the traditional interpretation of *helper*, so I told Dave I couldn't do it. I showed him the dictionary's take on the word to prove my point. "See," I said.

Dave listened intently, but he didn't seem nearly as alarmed as I was—or as he should be. Then he showed why he was so calm in the midst of my storm: "Have you looked up the Hebrew meaning of *helper*?" We had both been to seminary, but I had not taken Hebrew courses. Still, I knew how to look up words from the Old Testament's original language, so I did. In the Hebrew, *helper* meant something like "completer." I took my discovery to Dave, and, giving his best Tom Cruise impression from *Jerry Maguire*, he looked me in the eyes and said, "Ann, you complete me."

I'm not sure if you've seen the movie, but after this famous line, Renée Zellweger's character interrupts Jerry with, "Shut up. Just shut up." A long pause ensues as Jerry's hopes are dashed against the cruel rocks of rom-com reality. Then new hope sprung eternal as she tearfully yet joyfully continued, "You had me at hello."[1]

The problem with the idea of "you complete me" is that the man is still the central being in the relationship. He gets a helper to complete him, but the woman gets no such thing. I wanted someone to complete me too—and I had a hard time stomaching the idea that God didn't seem to really care about this need. Maybe you've been there too. If so, the good news is that there is more to *helper* than meets the eye.

"TOE THE LINE" OR "TOE-TO-TOE"?

Over the years, Genesis 2:18 has been a passage with many interpretations. But often, the simple interpretation of this verse in English does not capture what these words really meant when they were first spoken, and looking deeper into the original meaning allows us to see a divine character aligned with who we know our God to be.

Before we begin, you can relax; you don't have to be a scholar to go with me here. In fact, even scholars are still discovering new insights as they study these ancient words. The most humble and effective approach is to remember that just like our marriages, the ways God ordered his creation, including the genesis of the highly debated relational dynamics and patterns between men and women, didn't come out of nowhere. Again, this means that even in the mysteries surrounding ancient languages, we can trust that God was just as much God then as he is now—full of love, joy, peace, patience, and all the other aspects of the fruit of the Spirit. He hasn't changed, even as our understanding of him may shift.

We can engage these divinely inspired passages from thousands of years ago because they are informed by the character of God revealed through his Word and in the life of his Son Jesus. We can do a deep dive into these truths and principles, knowing that they are eternally present in our Creator and are for our good and for the good of our marriages even today. His goodness doesn't expire.

Over the years following my initial shock-and-awe response to the general interpretations of the word *helper* in Genesis 2:18, I continued to wrestle with the concept as a whole.

But along the way, God brought more scholars with deeper insights into my life. Dave and I have the honor of hosting a nationally syndicated radio show each week, so we get to sit down with a lot of incredible people. Much of what has helped shape new thoughts about *helpers* have been the conversations we've had with people around the table as we've laughed and shared meals together long after the radio interview is over.

Over one of those meals, we sat down with Kristi McLelland, an author and a professor who specializes in teaching people how to study the Bible for themselves through a Middle Eastern lens. I had to know what she thought about the interpretation of "a helper suitable for him" from Genesis 2:18. The original Hebrew words for the phrase are *ezer kenegdo.*

Kristi told us that many Jewish scholars don't interpret this phrase in terms of one member of the marriage being inferior or subservient to the other. Rather, the words denote strength like that of a warrior (Deuteronomy 33:7; Psalm 20:2). Let that sink in for a moment. Are you picturing yourself as a warrior in your beautiful armor? I liked princesses when I was a little girl, but as I got older, I felt the effects of the spiritual battle around me in my marriage and family. I began to feel the battle our culture was in. I realized I don't need a long, flowing dress. (Well, sometimes I do.) I need to put on the full armor of God.

Kristi went on to say that *ezer* is used twenty-one times in the Old Testament. Twice, it refers to Eve, the first woman. Another three times, it refers to powerful nations that came to *help* Israel when it was being besieged. But astoundingly, the other sixteen times refer to God as our helper. God is the one who comes alongside in our time of need. That is the true meaning of *ezer.* It was enlightening to learn this because I had been interpreting *helper* as a mere servant who performed boring, menial tasks. But in actuality, there is nothing subservient or inferior about being a helper. The term actually carries the idea of strengthening someone in a way they cannot do for themselves, which reveals a powerful understanding of God's unique strength and influence given to the woman.

The second part of the phrase—*kenegdo*, "suitable"—is where some people get stuck. This word is used only in Genesis 2, so we have no other examples to compare it to—which is why Kristi's insight blew my mind. She said that some Jewish scholars see the whole phrase more like "one who goes toe-to-toe with man." This doesn't mean the woman was made to fight or argue with the man, nor was she made to merely stand silent by his side while he does all the things that *really* matter in life. She is suitable because her strengths are shared with him, just as his strengths are shared with her. It's not one or the other, and, certainly, their strengths are not the same. Instead, there is an intermingling of the strengths given to each as an overflow of grace from their powerful and loving Creator. The two strengths become one over a lifetime—an active exchange of affection, words, ideas, ponderings, challenges (when merited), passions, and dreams.

Yes, *toe-to-toe* means that sometimes you and your spouse will contend with each other. There is conflict in marriage, which is probably one of the main reasons you're reading this book. The thing is, our husbands are also wearing armor—meaning, they have their own unique traits inherited from the Creator. Men and women are both warriors, and we are meant to battle alongside each other in the most epic battle of all—the spiritual battle. But instead of battling side by side, we often get mad at and disappointed in each other, turning to fight the one who is supposed to be our co-warrior in the fight. How our enemy must gloat with glee when we stop fighting him and start fighting our spouse instead. But in God's original design, even the differences between a woman and man were intended to be like iron sharpening iron for the betterment of both.

Sadly, the biblical phrase "iron sharpens iron" (Proverbs 27:17) is used today almost exclusively to describe men's strong camaraderie and accountability with other men. But women were made to be iron as well. Physical or emotional strengths or weaknesses aside, the origin of the idea of woman came from a divine expression of creating someone ready to go toe-to-toe with Adam.

Because God made us to stand toe-to-toe, it means we were not made to back down to the stronger one in the relationship. We have each been given strength exclusively by God. His strength in us is meant to be evident so that our strength will be a real toe-to-toe help to our husband.

As Kristi explained, *ezer kenegdo* shows us that we are not meant to be some man's little helper—his gofer—in life. To believe that is a great injustice not only toward women but also toward men who never get to feel the divine exhilaration and empowerment of a partner made by God to stand toe-to-toe with them.

HOW WE CHANGE EACH OTHER

Does this idea of being created to stand toe-to-toe with your man resonate with you? If you have been made to feel inferior, it may be too hard to believe right now, or it may offer you real relief, lighting a fire within you. Either way, take a breath and don't worry. You are safe here. But please take a minute to tell God all that these topics stir up in your heart. And then talk it out with other women you trust. Let God guide your thoughts and actions as you start to make a plan to go toe-to-toe—the right way—with your husband.

Remember, these concepts about *ezer kenegdo* find their origins and significance, not in man's interpretation of them, but in the God who spoke the words that literally brought the first woman to life. The value and strength that comes from him still make us come to life. If we try to accomplish change on our own, without God's help, we may rise up and exert our strength in a show of force, misinterpreting the truth of *ezer kenegdo* and hurting our husband in the process. Though it may feel good in the moment to exert your strength, God calls you to a different response, one that uplifts and encourages.

His ways can feel foolish when we first agree to follow them. But make no mistake, "the foolishness of God is wiser than human wisdom, and the weakness of God is stronger than human strength" (1 Corinthians 1:25). Our strength is not given to hurt, but to help. It is not meant to prove how strong we are, but to demonstrate the kind of strength God intends and that only he can give. This strength is about coming to grips with the beauty of divine truth, not finding justification to blame or attack—even if "human wisdom" says we have every right in the world to do so. Petty self-justifications and patterns of blaming are not signs of strength, not in God's kingdom at least.

Yes, in difficult moments and especially when we feel

mistreated, it is easy to freak out about what is happening *to us* or *around us*, but God wants us to focus more deeply on what is happening *within us*. Yes, God cares immensely about our troubles, but his chief goal in our lives is not to keep us insulated from all trouble or suffering. Jesus said as much in John 16:33: "In this world you will have trouble." Somehow we tend to miss this straightforward truth.

Trouble is a fact of life, but for most people today, avoiding any and all trouble has become an obsession. If a situation becomes hard or hurtful for us, we often feel justified to use our strength to hurt others in return. The trouble we experience makes it feel worth the trouble we cause.

Does God deliver us from trouble? Sure he does. All the time. But his highest, most gracious aim in our lives is not to keep us from all trouble; it's to shape us through every experience in life, including the troubled ones. God is less concerned about what we are *doing* and more concerned about who we are *becoming*. He is a good and gracious God who doesn't just let us know we will have trouble. He follows this difficult truth with a greater promise: "But take heart! I have overcome the world." You are not alone in this.

Two married people offer God one of his most potent tools for shaping each of them: marriage itself. And you as a woman have great power in the marriage, especially when it comes to your words. This goes beyond offering mere encouragement: "The words of the godly are a life-giving fountain" (Proverbs 10:11 NLT). When our words are aligned with God's ways, the result is nothing less than life itself—and not just a few drops, but a constantly overflowing fountain. When someone experiences this kind of life over and over again, they are changed forever. God uses your words to help form your husband into the man he is meant to be.

Dave and I had the chance to sit down with friends Dr. Jeff Myers, who holds a doctorate in theology, and Drew Dixon after their radio recordings to discuss the *ezer kenegdo* concept. We talked about the ever-present tension between men and women we all feel. In looking deeper into the original meaning of the phrase, Jeff and Drew talked about the tremendous power of the toe-to-toe concept and how it positions the man and the woman to face each other. I was excited about our conversation that day because I was eager to glean biblical insights from these gifted scholars.

After a few moments of conversation, Dr. Myers said something I will never forget: "You know what I think *ezer kenegdo* comes down to?" We all looked at him with anticipation. "I think when a man stands toe-to-toe with his wife and looks into her eyes, he sees the man he could become." There was silence in the room as the weight of his words fell on us. It felt like a holy moment. Tears sprang to my eyes as I contemplated what Dave had seen about himself when he looked at me during those early years of our marriage: Not enough. Passive. Always disappointing. Attention-seeking.

As I sat with Dr. Myer's words, another word stood out in my mind—*power*. As women, we hold so much power over our men's lives and their psyches that it can be scary and over-whelming. Yes, their identity comes from God, just as ours does, but he has set up the dynamics of marriage in such a way that we women hold a powerful missing piece to our husbands' puzzle of action and identity.

After that lunch conversation, Dave told me he was in total

agreement with Dr. Myers's assessment. He said that when he looks into my eyes and sees my affirmation and my belief in him, he begins to believe he can pretty much do anything. Why? Because when I go toe-to-toe with him—when I speak truth wrapped in encouragement or patiently continue to point out an important angle of a situation he is ignoring—God uses my strength to not only protect him, but also change him. It actually makes the two of us, as one, a powerful couple who can do significant kingdom work together.

But notice that this is the opposite of what the world thinks strength is—and of what I believed Dave needed from me for years. My love and respect for him are not concessions offered out of a defeated weakness; they are God-empowered choices that I'm able to make today because I have been allowing God to form me into his image through this process—not in my own strength, but in his. And God is using Dave to change me as well because I can now hear the wisdom and insight in his unique perspectives. Dave sees the beauty of my strength to love him well, and it does something to him that my nagging could never accomplish.

In the book of Proverbs, we read about the attributes of a virtuous wife of noble character (Proverbs 31:10–31). For years as a young woman, I didn't read Proverbs 31 because it made me feel so defeated. I thought I could never live up to the standards of that virtuous woman. But we often miss the beauty-creating-power context of this chapter. It begins in verse 1 with a shout-out to the person who taught the writer such wisdom—his mother. "The sayings of King Lemuel—an inspired utterance his mother taught him" (Proverbs 31:1).

She goes on to warn him of many things, including spending

time with the wrong women, but before she launches into a discourse on the beauty of the right woman, she appeals to his need to use his strength to pursue justice for the weak. "Speak up for those who cannot speak for themselves, for the rights of all who are destitute. Speak up and judge fairly; defend the rights of the poor and needy" (Proverbs 31:8–9). Though she is speaking directly to her son, there is an underlying truth offered to women: We can be used by God to help shape a man's actions so that he fights for the right causes rather than roaming about aimlessly, squandering his strength on things that don't help anyone.

Kristi McLelland told me how she sat with an elderly Jewish rabbi in Israel to talk about *ezer kenegdo*. He told her it seemed that since God knew there was an evil serpent (the enemy, Satan) in the garden, he knew it would take both women and men to eventually conquer the enemy. Yes, Jesus has already overcome the enemy, but he has chosen us to continue to fight with him through the grace of his victory until all things are reconciled, past and present, above and below. In these times, we stand shoulder to shoulder with our spouse in the fray, using our united strength.

Then there are those times when we walk straight into the unknown. In those moments, we walk hand in hand toward whatever lies before us. We can't see what's coming, but we can see each other and be confident that God has put us together to face the unknown with his help. In this, we see again how God is less concerned about where we're going than he is about who we are becoming. If life gets so dark or we become so lost that all we can see is each other, then by God's grace, we will be able to look into each other's eyes and see our future state of being glorified. Yes, we may not yet be perfected as we will be in heaven, but we can catch undeniable glimpses of eternity in the divine intimacy God has designed for us in our marriages here on earth. We can't yet escape to heaven, but heaven offers us someone here to laugh with, confide in, and to hold on to.

It comes down to fighting the right kinds of fights against a common enemy rather than each other. As we worry less about our power or roles and more about continuing to show up and respond to each other in love, we'll learn to practice gentle restraint so we're not tempted to say every single negative thing we feel like saying every time we want to say it.

In our culture, such restraint might feel like weakness or even injustice. However, Kristi McLelland brings the right perspective to our feelings about justice:

> Here in the West versus in the Middle East . . . when we think of justice, we think Lady Justice; and we think the scales, and we usually think of justice in terms of equality. But biblical justice is vertical; it's not horizontal. Biblical justice happens when the honorable reaches down to the shameful: lifts them out of their shame, restores their honor, and sends them forward in *shalom*.[2]

Real justice isn't only about fairness for ourselves, even though we often approach it that way. Ultimately, justice brings peace to those who need it the most or can't secure it for themselves. Every time Jesus encountered a woman, he lifted her up out of her shame and restored her honor and dignity. The next time you read the Gospels, look for his pattern. As Kristi beautifully points out, it will take your breath away.

Using our strength to choose words of life reveals true beauty to our husbands. King Lemuel's mother spells it out in Proverbs 31:10–12: "A wife of noble character who can find? She is worth far more than rubies. Her husband has full confidence in her and lacks nothing of value. She brings him good, not harm, all the days of her life." She concludes with the husband's praise of such a powerful woman: "Many women do noble things, but you surpass them all" (v. 29). Now that is praise I think any wife would like to hear!

God uses this beauty to spur on a husband to use his own strength for that which matters most—defending the weak and providing for the poor and vulnerable. When I saw my life-giving words transform my husband, I was encouraged to continue fighting the right kinds of fights with the security only Christ can give. This is how a new cycle of life in my marriage began, replacing the old patterns that brought death. And it's how a new cycle of life in your marriage can begin as well. Trust me, it's a life-giving fountain that will make you suitable helpers for each other in ways only God could dream up.

I didn't realize it then, but my mom knew more than a little about being the right kind of helper, though I had always seen her as a doormat. My parents were married seventy years and finally became believers. My mom became devoted to Jesus after my sister and I became believers, though it took my dad quite a bit longer. So don't stop praying for those you love.

For the last thirteen years of her life, my mom struggled with Alzheimer's. One of the most inspiring things I ever witnessed was watching my dad care for my mom. For most of my life, I saw my dad as a self-centered husband who took his wife for granted. But my mom just kept loving him, serving him, believing in him, and cheering for him. Yes, it seemed unjust to me. And yes, my dad should have done better. But after all those years, I eventually watched him do absolutely everything for my mom. He rubbed lotion on her arms. He cooked her food. He did all of the laundry. He cleaned the house. These were things I had never seen him do before.

One day, I said to him, "Dad, I respect you so much. You take such good care of Mom. You are her most committed helper in the world."

Tears welled up in his eyes. "How could I not be? She's my partner—she's my girl." My eyes filled with tears as he continued, "She has loved me so well her whole life. How could I not do the same for her? She has made me who I am."

I thought my mom was weak for being the kind of helper she was. But later in life, my dad told me how she would come to him and always speak her mind in private when it mattered and when the kids weren't around. She would still be respectful but direct. She was no doormat. She had incredible strength. I just didn't understand it at the time. Now I want to be a powerful helper like she was.

DAVE'S REFLECTION

Wow! I am still tearing up after reading Ann's words about her mom and dad. I used to challenge her dad to be more respectful of her mom, but he didn't seem to understand what I was saying. But when she struggled with dementia, he completely changed. He was a better man because she had been a true *ezer kenegdo* to him.

Ann has done the same for me. She stands beside me as my fellow warrior in the spiritual battle, but she has also stood toe-to-toe with me when I needed it. I remember how Ann challenged me when our youngest son was getting ready to head to college on a football scholarship. We bought him a new laptop for his college years, and as we were about to give it to him, Ann said to me, "You are an amazing writer. It would probably be super reassuring to Cody to receive an email from you to encourage him as he walks into freshman football camp next week." She didn't scold me or shame me into writing him, but rather cheered me on and challenged me to do something I wouldn't have done without her encouragement.

So I wrote the email to Cody, encouraging him to not give up when football became hard. I told him of the number of times I wanted to quit football during my college years. I never heard a word back from Cody about that email over those four years of school. I wasn't even sure he had read it. But when he graduated, he sent the email back to me and said, "Thanks, Dad. I read this email almost every day for the past four years, and it kept me going when I wanted to quit."

I bet you're smiling right now because you know I never

would have written that email without Ann's challenge and encouragement. I know it too. And I also know that if she had shamed me into doing it, either it never would have happened or would have been poorly done.

We are grown men, but in many ways on the inside, we're just little boys who are looking for encouragement. When we are challenged in an encouraging "I believe in you" way, we want to rise up and seek greatness. When that same son was headed to training camp for his shot in the NFL, guess who sent him another email? You know why. Ann was standing toe-to-toe with me.

As Ann so beautifully proved with her own approach toward me, all things are truly possible with God working in us.

CHAPTER 4

CHANGING THOUGHT PATTERNS

Don't copy the behavior and customs of this world,
but let God transform you into a new person by
changing the way you think.

ROMANS 12:2 NLT

If you're like me, you have a constant internal dialogue
going on in your head. I'm not necessarily talking to
myself. I'm just always thinking in unspoken words.
Did you know we actually say more words to ourselves
than to other people? Most of us do this kind of thinking without, well, thinking. And since we all do it, it's
very easy to overlook the power of those words rolling
around in our head, even if they never find their way
out of our mouth.

Much of the change in my life after "the Great
Boo" came from my willingness to examine my thought

69

patterns. I would like to take credit for this, but when I asked God if I booed Dave, I felt like he was prompting me to start paying attention to my thoughts. I'm embarrassed to talk about this, so again, I can't take credit.

Before I started examining my thoughts, I was stuck in a negative thought pattern about Dave. For instance, while I was ironing clothes or mowing the lawn, I was performing a long-form monologue inside my head on the topic "How Dave Gets Everything Done for Work but Doesn't Do the Things Needed at Home." The short title was: "How Dave Keeps Failing Me." And let me tell you, I had those lines memorized. But until Dave called out my booing and the Lord led me to truly examine my thoughts, I didn't know I was rehearsing the same script over and over again. It just happened on autopilot.

Yes, I know it's hard to evaluate a certain thing (your brain) using the same thing you are evaluating (your brain). It's a little like giving yourself a lie detector test. Depending on how you are wired, your mind can play tricks, convincing you that something either really isn't *that bad*, is *way worse* than it really is, or *doesn't even exist* in the first place, especially if you're prone to undue guilt or an exaggerated sense of blame of others. Your mind will always be searching for something to feel shame over or someone who should be held responsible. Getting to know your own mind better takes work, but it's good work.

Learning to mind the business of your mind with honesty and accuracy requires you to invite outside information and sources. The idea is to keep yourself from inadvertently duping yourself as if you were in the fourteenth hour of the movie *Inception* (no, it wasn't that long; it just felt that way).

You need help from sources outside of yourself—trusted friends, a church community, therapists, who will help you more rightly evaluate yourself, even showing you where you can more confidently trust your own opinions of yourself and where you certainly cannot.

Now I want to show you some of the truly remarkable ways that what you think about your husband affects your life, and his, in more ways than you, well, think.

WHAT PEOPLE MADLY IN LOVE ARE REALLY THINKING

When Dave and I were engaged, I was absolutely head over heels for him. I couldn't even think about him without that wonderful butterfly feeling in my stomach. He could make me feel all jittery with just a look. Everything he said was the funniest thing I'd ever heard. There was no one else I wanted to spend the rest of my life with. Dave was *my* man.

It begs the question: How can one go from such a state of constant relational euphoria to a state of constant inner complaining—and all over the exact same person? Some of it has to do with expectations we have for marriage that begin forming even in childhood. These expectations deeply inform our thought patterns in profound ways.

I grew up with an inner expectation to be the best at everything. As an eleven-year-old, I remember coming home from a regional gymnastics meet with a third-place ribbon in the "All Around" category. I had placed and medaled in all events. I was ecstatic! My dad had good intentions, but the words that came out of his mouth crushed me: "We are the Barons; we are the best. Never be satisfied with anything but first place and don't bother coming home unless you are the winner." Of course, he played it off like he was joking, but a certain neural pathway was paved in my brain that day, lined with one-way street signs that all read, "Be Perfect or You're Going the Wrong Way."

Had my dad made any comments about marriage? No. But he didn't have to. We all bring to our marriages the thought patterns we developed in childhood and adolescence. We don't have to try—we are already doing it. I wonder what patterns and pathways you have carried into your marriage.

For me, a life of intense performance pressure had led me to develop certain subconscious perceptions and expectations of what marriage should be. In my mind, Dave Wilson was going to be my first-place trophy, the completion of every part of my life. He would be everything to me that my dad couldn't be. He was going to be a pastor, after all. He would woo me every day of our marriage, just as he had done when we started dating. He would listen to my needs and lead me and our kids into spiritual and emotional maturity. He was my ticket to the life I had felt the pressure to attain for years. I would finally win the guy, and the credits would roll at the end of our romantic story. I didn't walk into marriage knowing I had any of these expectations. I just wanted a good marriage that reflected Jesus. But my disappointments and feeling of being let down by Dave revealed the hidden expectations of my heart.

The problem was, I wasn't ready for someone to turn the lights on and tell me I had to leave my mental theater and enter the real world. Sure, the popcorn was better, but I digress. I didn't know that my brain had already mapped out a completely self-destructive course of thinking without my knowledge or consent. Brains will do that sometimes. Obviously, Dave was never going to be able to fill the God-sized hole in my psyche, including my deeply embedded internal centers of intimacy and security.

Having talked to women in all different kinds of circumstances for more than thirty years, I can tell you that such monumental expectations often derail marriages, or at least leave the wife attempting to pull her husband up to the lofty standards of her original expectations. What expectations did you have of your husband? My brain thought if I could just change Dave into the husband I thought I had married, then I would be happy. So then, while men are equally at fault and the incessant booing of their wives seems to be well deserved, it is also equally true that misplaced, unmet, unrealistic expectations in the mind of the woman are, at best, contributing to her pain. At worst, her thought patterns are doing more damage than what she perceives her husband is doing.

As it turns out, if we don't learn to recognize and lead our repetitive thoughts, they will lead us where we don't want to go—and we won't even know we're going there. A favorite guest on *FamilyLife Today* is speaker and author Ted Lowe, who has taught me so much about what's going on inside our heads and how it affects marriage. His book *Us in Mind* is a masterpiece on the topic.[1]

Ted dove deep into a brain-scan study about happily married couples conducted by Dr. Helen Fisher. Well, "happily married" doesn't do it justice. Dr. Fisher went straight for the gusto and tracked down couples, married for an average of twenty-one years, who could both honestly say they were "madly in love" with their spouse. Instead of just searching for what makes things go wrong, which is easy to find in every online video or teaching on marriage (ours included), Dr. Fisher set out to discover what makes the best marriages go right.[2]

She studied three areas of the brain with varying observable activity under certain conditions. One area is responsible for a phenomenon called "positive illusion"—that is, the ability to focus on what you *do* like about your spouse instead of what you *don't* like about them. Now, before we get to the part where you argue that such an approach feels like denying reality (after all, the word *illusion* is in the name), just know that the data doesn't lie. Partners with high levels of positive illusion truly do report higher marital satisfaction, less conflict, and a higher sense of security and lasting intimacy. They look at their spouse and see everything about them that they love and that is good.[3]

Conversely, unhappily married couples tend to focus on what they *don't love* about their spouse. It is such an easy thing to do. When I was disgruntled with Dave, I could be folding clothes and fixating on Dave's negatives, replaying them repeatedly in my mind. It was not just the moment after the boo story that changed the way I think. God had to deal with me for a long time on this front. After all, I had been thinking a certain way for well over a decade. I wasn't just going to start thinking differently overnight. Changing thought patterns takes time. In fact, God still deals with me about them. It's a lifelong journey toward ways of thinking that are more reflective of who we are in Christ rather than who we feel we are in our daily lives.

This is not about being delusional or putting yourself in harm's way. But outside of tragic or unhealthy extremes, most of us tend to think this way—to hyperfocus on all the things we *don't* love about our spouse. In these moments, our thoughts can slip into "confirmation bias." This means we begin finding exactly what we're looking for in our spouse.[4]

I can remember such moments of confirmation bias quite vividly. They were a daily way of life. I believed the worst about Dave, so even when he did a chore or came home early from work, I wasn't satisfied because I couldn't see past what I was already believing about him to actually see what he was doing. The chore was never done properly—after all, since he rarely did it, he really didn't even know how to do it. Can you see how I looked past what he was actually doing to believe what I already wanted to believe about him?

When confirmation bias becomes a true pattern of thought in our brains, we begin to sound like children rather than adults—with a childish catchphrase: "just because." *You are playing with the kids just because you feel bad for being gone so much, not because you really want to be present. You are complimenting my outfit just because you want to have sex, not because you really think I'm pretty. You are unloading the dishes just because you don't want me to be mad at you—and you're not even doing it right!*

This last one is a real indicator that we're not thinking clearly. Have you ever done this? What significant motivation would we want our husband to have about doing the dishes? Do we want him to love it out of principle? We probably don't love it either, but we don't criticize ourselves for it. Do we want him to do the dishes to take a task off us so we can be together? Perhaps, but even if he does it because he doesn't want to make us mad, isn't this kind of the same thing? Don't we all desire to keep the people we love from becoming angry at us? And besides that, what kind of mindset must we be in if our husband knows that even if he does the very thing we want him to do, it can still lead to criticism or conflict? That's some complicated overthinking right there.

Negative confirmation bias is very powerful; once it sets in, trust me, your husband won't be able to do anything right. He will prove you right about his wrongness every single day—it will be so obviously cut-and-dried. Every attempt to make things better or lack of attempt, perhaps not made because he knows he'll fail you, will add evidence for the conclusion you've already made. At that point, it really won't matter what he does in reality, because the reality in your head will always be more real than anything else.

The most profound part of a negative confirmation bias is that it can contribute to the very thing you say you are upset about. The Arbinger Institute calls this "collusion." Yes, when your heart is at war with your spouse so that a negative confirmation bias dictates what you think and believe about him, you actually collude with him against yourself. In your mind, he is no longer your husband—a person you consciously love and in whom you can see some positive value. Instead, he is merely another obstruction blocking your way and causing trouble. He has become a common object tethered to a negative adjective—lazy father, deadbeat husband, helpless child, and so forth.

Once someone becomes an object in our minds rather than a real human being, we will feel justified in treating them any way we want because we've stripped them of their humanity. After all, the regular internal processes that make us decent adults and humans—the constant consideration of another human's humanity—have been forfeited.[5] The result is that we stop feeling a responsibility to consider their motivations, intentions, or the need for mercy that every human has many times over every single day. We don't care how their day went. We can only consider how ours is going.

And guess what? When we treat people like this, especially our spouse, they will respond as if they are being mistreated because, well, they are. But in a state of confirmation bias that has led to full-on collusion, we can see only *their* negatives. *Our* negatives are justified; thus, there is no need to consider them. Yet somehow we are shocked when our husband continues the exact behaviors we dehumanized him for, even though it's actually exactly what we should have expected. "When we start seeing others as objects," writes the Arbinger researchers, "we begin provoking them to make our lives difficult. We actually start inviting others to make us miserable. We begin provoking in others the very things we say we hate."[6]

It's a horribly sad state to be in. I know from firsthand experience. I was in that rut, colluding with my husband against myself, but I had no idea it had become a well-worn pattern. Your spouse can never win in these situations. Please take a moment to read the Arbinger quote in the paragraph above because it is well worth working to truly understand it.

When I first read about negative confirmation bias, I thought, *How would I feel if our sons' wives did this to them?*

I have amazing daughters-in-law who are so much better at focusing on the things they like about their husbands than I ever was. And I would feel so heartbroken if they couldn't see the greatness in my sons. Sometimes it helps to imagine focusing on negatives happening to someone else you dearly love. And when you grasp it, you will be taking the first step toward real change.

I'm not saying your husband isn't doing wrong things or simply isn't doing the right things. Either of these may be true. I'm only saying that no matter how justified your negative feelings are in your head, what he is doing is not the only thing that's true. His actions are not denying you the ability to choose your reactions. The research is clear, whether we like it or not, couples who are madly in love are not simply married to better people; they are instead choosing to concentrate on what they love about the other. On the whole, couples stop being madly in love because they become beekeepers of a dangerous hive of negativity. They may call their spouse "honey," but there is little sweetness in their thoughts about their spouse.

I used to think Dave lived in a delusional world because he saw our marriage as great—and he told me he also saw me as great. I used to tell him that he saw things that way because he avoided conflict and didn't want to face reality. What a negative thing to say to him! These days, I'm realizing what a gift his perspective was to me and to our marriage. He was on the positive path, which was necessary since I was on the negative path so often.

Why does this happen to us so easily? Why are negative thoughts so much more prevalent than positive thoughts? And how do we begin to make changes to our thought patterns that can bring us back to the good kind of mad love?

WHY SO NEGATIVE?

Ted Lowe talks about how our thoughts are not our actions or attitudes. However, they do inform and shape what both will become. The way we think inclines us toward a way of being. It's easy to look at Scripture and think that it only tells us how to speak or act, but the truth is, there is so much in God's Word that urges us to be aware of our thoughts.

Isaiah says that where we direct our thoughts determines how much peace we experience: "You will keep in perfect peace those whose minds are steadfast, because they trust in you" (Isaiah 26:3). Paul echoes this exact sentiment in Romans 8:6 (NLT): "So letting your sinful nature control your mind leads to death. But letting the Spirit control your mind leads to life and peace." The English Standard Version uses the expression "to set the mind on" fleshly, negative things. This an interesting way to think about it. The mind may feel like it's constantly wandering with or without our consent, kind of like drifting off to sleep when you just can't keep your eyes open. But we have been given the power to set our minds on different things, like setting an alarm clock that awakens us to right ways of thinking each day.

We don't have to be a slave to our own mind. God's Spirit promises to help us break free from old thought patterns if we will lean into his grace and his ways over time. It certainly begins with honesty about our thought struggles, but it doesn't end there. God doesn't leave us to our own devices. He doesn't ask sick people to perform their own surgeries. No, he is at work in us: "God is working in you, giving you the desire and the power to do what pleases him" (Philippians 2:13 NLT).

You see, he doesn't just work to alter our behaviors. His

deepest work is seen in transforming our thoughts, motivations, and desires, so that ultimately we become like Christ. He knows that if we allow him to fully release our potential, we can do incredible things for his kingdom. He doesn't want us to be complacent or resigned to an insignificant life. There is so much more he wants to give us if we will say yes to the hard work of soul change.

Jesus knew what his disciples were thinking and talked with them about it. He didn't leave them alone to think and do the wrong things. He challenged them because he knew that their thoughts were important enough to be known, evaluated, and, when necessary, completely changed. He wants the same for us. Our thoughts should mirror his: "In your relationships with one another, have the same mindset as Christ Jesus" (Philippians 2:5). But who can do such a thing—you know, think like Jesus thinks?

No one can, without some help that is. It's a good thing we have the Holy Spirit, our Helper, who is by far a better helper than the "helper" I thought I was to Dave. God's Word shows us exactly how our thoughts can be changed: "Finally, brothers and sisters, whatever is true, whatever is noble, whatever is right, whatever is pure, whatever is lovely, whatever is admirable—if anything is excellent or praiseworthy—think about such things" (Philippians 4:8).

Now that's a direct statement that removes all ambiguity and doubt about what we should do. We often think that being told what to do brings confinement, but in actuality, when we trust the One who is being direct with us because we truly believe he knows better than us, it brings complete freedom. When we know exactly what we're supposed to do, we can stop all the angst and wasted time pondering what we should do. Instead, we are granted the grace of clarity: *Hey you—yes, you there under the pile of laundry. Right now, I want you to think about these things, not those other things. Also, next time, don't forget the dryer sheets.*

The New Testament in Modern English (PHILLIPS) uses the phrase "fix your minds" in Philippians 4:8—an interesting internal image of intentionally affixing your mind to concepts and ideas that are not already there. It is the difference between lying back and letting the currents of your naturally negative thoughts take you where they will or grabbing a rope thrown to you by a passing boat.

The boat is Spirit-led thinking that counters the currents of negativity all around you. Holding tightly to the rope is an intentional act that requires only the grip strength of a simple faith that takes hold over and over again. In the end, the boat is doing the real work—that is, the Spirit leads us into right thinking if we will only fix our minds on his ways. The coolest part? When we are pulled against the current by a power greater and faster than our own, we rise above the waves as the resistance of God-based positive thinking causes us to ski on the surface of negativity all around us.

But why are negative thoughts as vast as the ocean and positive thoughts so hard to come by? At first glance, we're tempted to say that negative thoughts are more prevalent because they better reflect reality—that is, we think negative things about our husband because he is actually doing or not doing things in a negative way. *So, take that, Philippians 4:8! You want me to think on things that are true, eh? That's exactly what I'm doing My husband is truly selfish and manipulative!*

We will deal with this particular conundrum in a few pages, but before we do, let's talk a bit more about how our seemingly conclusive perceptions of negative truths may not be as conclusive as they seem. We tend to assume that the negative thoughts in our lives are merely normal, justifiable reflections of all the negative things happening to us. I'm not saying negative things don't happen, but there's more to it than that. Humanity has been temporarily rewired for negativity in a way that Adam and Eve wouldn't have fathomed before their epic fall into the sinful state that we've all been falling into ever since. Your husband may be doing something truly negative, but before he ever did, you were already prone to thinking negative things.

Research supports this idea of the unequal power of negativity in our minds. Psychologist and professor emeritus John Gottman studied positive and negative interactions between couples to determine ratios and their significance with respect to the health of their marriage. What they learned was astounding. These ratios could predict divorce or stability with uncanny accuracy. The variable? Positive and negative thought and communication patterns.

Couples who were stable approached communication and conflict without abandoning positivity toward their partner. Even when arguing, they still did things like ask questions, be kind, show affection, and be empathetic to what their partner might be feeling, even in disagreement. On the negative side, couples whose communication and conflict included constant criticism, hostility, harsh words, and the sense that their spouse was a problem to be solved were much more likely to be headed toward relational despair, including divorce.[7]

Okay, this probably seems like common sense. Of course, it seems obvious that happy couples have positive interactions, and unhappy couples have negative ones. But that actually isn't the most insightful part of the study. Gottman stumbled upon a "magic ratio" of positive to negative in relationships that stay together: five to one. In other words, in healthy relationships, there are five times as many positive relational things going on than negative dynamics or patterns. The implications are huge. If we hurt our partner's feelings by saying or doing something negative, it takes five positive things to make up for it and bring the relationship back to equilibrium.[8]

That is the power of negativity. It takes up more space in our brains—five times more space—than the positive, to be exact. The negative causes more pain and inflicts more damage than the positive, which may explain why it feels so much harder to overlook the negative and find the positive when it comes to your spouse. This is simply your brain at work in a fallen world.

Doesn't this make sense in your experience at work or home? When I speak at a conference, I can get twenty-five wonderful comments and one negative one. If you're like me, I remember only the negative one. And if you have any performance issues in your past like I do, you will *especially* remember the negative. Even if you don't have these kinds of stories in your past, you may still have a hard time forgetting even one negative comment.

If our words shape our worlds, what kind of atmosphere have we created in our homes? Our words start with a thought, which can be a scary reality to accept. But it can also lead to amazing things if we accept it and grow into better places.

THE BIG "WHAT IF"

Let's return now to the question, "What if my husband really is doing all these negative things?" Perhaps talking about seeing your husband in a more positive light can begin to feel like denial. One of my greatest fears of changing my negative thinking about Dave when he wasn't measuring up to my expectations was that I would enable him to continue in his bad behavior. In my mind, he would just think, *Ooh, she's finally happy, so I don't have to worry about getting any better!* As I said before, I was withholding my praise because everybody else was praising him as a pastor at church, as a chaplain with the Detroit Lions, and as a speaker. I only wish I'd known that my affirmation was more powerful than all the rest of theirs combined—and my negativity was also five times more potent. With all of the negative things I perceived about Dave, I didn't really see the point in looking for anything good.

Over the years, I've spoken on this topic at various events, and every time, a few women approach me afterward to tell me they can't think of anything praiseworthy about their husbands. I remember one woman in particular who was beside herself. "You don't understand," she said, with tears filling her eyes. "There's literally nothing positive about him that I can affirm. Do you want me to be a Hollywood actress? I mean, what if there's no good there to find?"*

I understand that as you face this big "what if," it can be

---

*I can't say it enough times that I am not talking about those who are being emotionally, physically, or sexually abused. In these instances, you can stop looking for the good in your abuser and start looking for a way out of the dangerous situation you are in.

discouraging and daunting. In humility and gentleness, I will tell you what I told the woman at the event and many others like her. "I know it's hard to see the good in your husband right now, because he hasn't shown you in a long time that there is anything to believe in. But try to go back in time to when you were dating or when you were first married. I guarantee that you saw something in him back then—something good that made him worth marrying. It's a way to take action toward the positive illusion you once experienced. It's not easy and it takes work, but I'm here to tell you it can happen."

In Revelation 2:4–5 (NLT), the apostle John addresses a church that has lost its first love for God. He's trying to encourage them to get that love back. "But I have this complaint against you. You don't love me or each other as you did at first! Look how far you have fallen! Turn back to me and do the works you did at first." The same concept can be applied to our marriages. We can lose a sense of our early love that was once so strong. But we can also return to this early love and once again find the good we saw so easily in the beginning.

If you feel stuck in apathy or hopelessness, try to move out of it as quickly as possible. Apathy and hopelessness are like wet concrete. If left alone, they will soon set and harden. If you want to get rid of them later on, it will take a jackhammer instead of a bucket. What do you do when someone has been unfaithful to you? When they have broken their promises? When they keep saying they will change but never do? There are no good answers, and the Bible gives guidance for abandoning a marriage. I'm not telling you to stay no matter what; I'm saying that before you check out emotionally, maybe try to change the way you're thinking about him. Yes, he will eventually have to meet you in the middle. But for now, it may not be time to give up. A good counselor can help, even if you have to go alone.

If you can't get yourself to recall anything good about your husband, you can try something else—find the good in him that comes because he is made in God's image. Yes, he may not look or act like what you think someone made in God's image would look or act like, but God still loves him as a son—even if he's in a pigpen a far way off. Regardless, God's heart is to celebrate his son—to cheer for him. This is exactly what the father in Luke 15 did when his wayward son returned home. This guy had really screwed things up, but the father's love reached beyond his mistakes and betrayal.

No, you are not God, and no one is asking you to be. But perhaps the last stone you haven't turned over when it comes to finding something good about your husband is the one related to his value before God. This does not let him off the hook; it lets you find hope in God's mindset, so that you don't have to carry the weight of the constant mistakes and shortcomings of someone you love but can't bring yourself to encourage. In these "what if"" moments, you can start by confidently affirming the value God has given your husband. Here are a couple of things you might consider saying to him:

> *I know you're not perfect, but you were made for good things, and I'm excited to see how they all come to fruition.*
> *You are so creative and you work so hard.*
> *You do a great job of physically protecting us, and I appreciate that about you.*
> *You are loved and valued.*

I was just thinking about how you are the only man I ever wanted to marry.

Some of these may seem like a stretch to you; they would have been for me at first too. I had to start simple: "Thanks for getting the oil changed in the car." But that's where it started— with my mind being informed by God's thoughts about Dave more than my own. I began to realize that no matter what I was feeling, I could look at Dave and choose to see in him what the Scriptures reveal that God sees in him. The best part is that I also began seeing more of what God sees in me—a daughter who is delighted in by her Father. It brought me comfort to know that I was seen by God, even if I didn't feel seen by Dave.

Without any denial of our reality, I began thinking, by God's grace, in ways that gave me permission to stop carrying the huge weight of pain and injustice all by my lonesome. Instead, I began partnering with God, and the weight soon started to get lighter and lighter. Over time, I began not just to see what God sees about Dave, but also to believe it, even if he couldn't yet believe it for himself. His strengths were being eclipsed by my negative biases, things hidden and lost in the difficult years of our marriage. Finding them wasn't about lying to myself, but rather about believing the truth of what God says about Dave.

I began calling out in Dave what he had forgotten about himself—strengths, gifts, ways of being in the world, a uniqueness no one else had. These were all things I once saw, but that had become buried, one at a time, with every five piles of mud I inadvertently threw on him, staining each clean spot in his character and confidence. And yes, he had done the same to me. There was no doubt. But I learned it wasn't going to be his perfect alignment with my expectations that would make this thing work. I had to become aligned with a higher truth about God, myself, and Dave.

Yes, there was the chance that Dave would not reciprocate, or wouldn't do so for a long time. Taking a chance was scary, but since I was no longer trying to fix my husband as much as I was trying to fix my thoughts on Jesus, Dave's imperfections stopped being stones tied around my emotional neck that could so easily pull me to the bottom. Instead, I began to see the parts of Dave that God made to be good and endearing begin to rise to the surface.

I began to pray every day, "Show me the greatness of Dave." After all, I knew that if God had crafted my husband, then greatness most definitely lay within him. Over time, it felt like God gave me new eyes to see his passion, courage, loyalty, work ethic, spiritual hunger, humor, humility, and so much more. And ever since, I've had a heart for women and men in these situations. I want women to see the good in their men, the way I now see the strength and goodness in Dave. I want truthful, honest, helpful, healing labels applied to our men.

I am the mom of three grown sons, so I feel more than a little concerned about the way men are seen in our culture today. They are too often dismissed as stupid, irresponsible Neanderthals who can't even pack a sack lunch correctly. They are labeled power hungry and accused of fostering oppressive systems. Our expectations of men have become so low. So guess what? They live up to them—or should I say, down to them. And though they are made in God's image with unique gifts and qualities, we continue to denigrate and compare them. And it's killing their confidence to show up and be present in the courageous work of loving their families well and fighting against injustice in the world, which just perpetuates the cycle.

No, we shouldn't stand by and do nothing about abusive patriarchal attitudes and systems that hurt women. No, we can't stop men from self-destructing. Yes, many men have done a lot of damage. Still, seeing only the negatives in the man we're married to isn't actually making him or us become better. The Scriptures and brain science are in alignment on this: Spending our time and energy obsessively thinking about all the ways our man is failing isn't helping him. And it isn't helping us either.

Instead, it makes perfect sense that God wants to use us to unleash in our husbands the love, joy, peace, patience, kindness, goodness, faithfulness, gentleness, and self-control that the Spirit has imparted to them (Galatians 5:23 ESV). God wants to change our husbands for good—a change that may start only when we transform the way we think about them.

DAVE'S REFLECTION

The research Ann discovered about the power behind how and what we think really blew my mind. There are a lot of brain references, I know. But the research holds true. I've witnessed it firsthand. When Ann heard God's invitation to see the world and our marriage differently, she became willing to let him change the ways she was thinking about me. And that change in her thinking began to create new neurological pathways—some call them "brain ruts"—in her brain.

As she started to encourage me more and more, even when she told me something I needed to do differently, it helped me see the man I needed to become. Her cheering me on—not her excessive criticism—was the real help I needed. It also had another unexpected effect. I not only knew who I needed to become, but I began to truly want to be that man too. I was able to make strides toward becoming that man in ways I never could before.

God's loving honesty toward Ann reshaped her thoughts, and God used the kindness and respect Ann offered me out of those changes to reshape the disposition and desires of my heart. I became kinder, more present, engaged, and willing to try to show up for our life together. When both partners humble themselves, listen, and become open to change, even though our world sees that as losing, the truth is that everyone in the relationship wins.

One study that Ann didn't talk about accentuates everything she has already said. In New York, Dr. Sandra Murray coauthored a study that had couples rank their partners in several positive categories.[9] They evaluated their spouse on qualities such as how kind and affectionate they were, how open and disclosing, how patient, how warm, how sociable, and the like. The results were quite astounding.

Most people would assume that the happiest couples are those who are on the same page about each other's strengths and weaknesses. This feels like authentic honesty to us, and in our modern culture, the perception of authenticity is one of the highest ideals, if not *the* highest. We avoid fake at all costs. However, this study had something else to say about what makes a fulfilled marriage.

The happiest and most satisfied married people rated their partner more positively than their partner rated themselves. And they did so in every one of the categories of the study. The research revealed that, on its own, the act of fully knowing each other's strengths and weaknesses doesn't make couples any happier. Rather, writes Ted Lowe, "the people who saw their partner as better than they saw themselves—or love-blind couples—were happiest. In other words, a happy marriage was made up of two people who thought of each other, 'I wish you could see you the way I see you.'"[10]

That's exactly what Ann did for me. She began thinking of me better than I thought of myself. Note that this doesn't mean she no longer saw my flaws. She just chose to shift her focus to the good things in me and encouraged me to see them too. I don't know exactly how she did it, but I know that God was the One working in both of us. As it turns out, our inherited image of God makes us more resilient and able to change than we may think. Brain science and relationship research confirm this divine truth. Dr. Murray attests, "People are very good at changing their definitions to match how they want to see themselves or how they want to see others."[11]

This reminds me of a Scripture that leads directly to these truths. Romans 12:10 (ESV) says we should "outdo one another in showing honor." Isn't it crazy that the same truth the world is now discovering has been in the Bible the whole time? When marriage is a relationship where we outdo one another with honorable thoughts and beliefs, both partners win. Also, both partners are more likely to grow over time to look more like the person their spouse already sees better than they can.

The concept is also reflected in the way God sees us and changes our lives by inviting us to look honestly at his glory—that is, the limitless brightness of his goodness, mercy, and strength. "And we all, with unveiled face, beholding the glory of the Lord, are being transformed into the same image from one degree of glory to another. For this comes from the Lord who is the Spirit" (2 Corinthians 3:18 ESV). The longer we look at what is glorious about God, the more our lives will reflect that glory.

Finally, Philippians 2:3 (NLT) sums up these truths in a simple way: "Don't be selfish; don't try to impress others. Be humble, *thinking of others as better than yourselves*" (emphasis mine). In my marriage, I always knew that Ann was better than me (most husbands know it's true for them too), but my insecurity kept me from honoring her as if I believed it. Instead, I wallowed in self-pity and pride, feeling that I could never measure up to her or to her standards for me. And every time she criticized me for it, I just swam down deeper into the same feelings. But when God began to change her thoughts about me, he also began changing my thoughts about her. Over time, we both rediscovered the joy of being more love-blind toward the other's faults and more wide-eyed to the truths that mattered.

This can be true for you too. As you lean into becoming more encouraging toward your husband, you'll still know his faults are there, but you'll get so busy enjoying the good God-imaged characteristics in him (and hopefully he in you) that you won't have much time or energy anymore to focus on the negative.

CHAPTER 5

RESPECT: THE NEW REBELLION

If you do good to those who are good to you, what credit is that to you? Even sinners do that.

LUKE 6:33

We all love a good underdog story, whether true or fictionalized, about someone who dares to stand up and do the right thing, like the American colonists telling King George III where he could stick his taxes on tea—in the Boston Harbor, to be exact. Harriet Tubman escaping from brutal bondage in the South, only to defiantly sneak back into the land of her slavery more than a dozen times to lead many others to freedom. Or when Skye realizes the great power she has, even as the smallest of all the Paw Patrols, as she goes on to defeat the mad scientist (that's for you moms who feel like you've lost a few brain cells but still love your kids—and for you grandmas who would watch anything just to hang with your grandkids).

In today's world, rebelling against injustice is a common mantra. *Speak truth to power, stand up for what you believe, and don't back down.* Let me be clear, when it comes to real injustice in the world—slavery, trafficking, predatory behaviors, and the like—we should absolutely rebel against whatever or whomever perpetuates the injustice.

But apart from taking action against these kinds of injustices, what if I told you that the most rebellious thing you could do in your normal, everyday life is to be kind, respectful, and grateful? There have been times in our history when common courtesy was an expectation, even if not everyone met it. But now, it's as though we've rewritten the very foundations of our values, elevating disrespect as if it were a virtue. Take these for example:

> *You should just tell your boss off—he deserves it!*
> *We've been waiting fifteen minutes for our meal—no tip for this waitress!*
> *This guy is doing 70 miles per hour in the freaking fast lane—get in the slow lane, dude!*

We seem to be drawn to the idea of taking others down a peg, as if doing so is a positive expression of strength. Again, there are times when standing up to a bully or a tyrant is absolutely the right thing to do, especially when it's on behalf of the poor, the neglected, or the marginalized. But we've gone way past such noble missions. Our culture seems to openly disrespect and then exclusively self-protect. The proof is easy to find. If we perceive that someone in our "trusted" group has wronged us in any way, we attack them just as harshly as we do any old stranger on the road or on the internet. If we feel disrespected, we no longer feel obligated to show respect.

When it comes to social media, we've gone so far as a society (including a high percentage of Christians) to feel not only justified but also morally righteous in blasting anyone who dares to offer an opposing viewpoint or, dare I say it, a negative comment on one of our posts. This makes my heart sad. I've gotten to the point where I don't even read some of the comments on social media anymore because people can be downright cruel to one another.

It's no wonder that in this sort of environment of heightened negative thought and communication, the good in others can be so easily dismissed and people quickly canceled because of their "mistakes." It is no longer enough to respectfully disagree—in fact, if you begin a sentence using the words "with all due respect," it is almost a certainty that what you are about to say will be "without any due respect." Why? The clue is in the phrase. We no longer think most people are "due any respect" from us. And if they aren't due, anything they do simply won't do. So we can say anything we want about them or even to them.

Nowadays, offering real respect to someone is a rebellious act because it sets us apart from the attitudes and actions of most people in the world—and, unfortunately, in many marriages.

But what if the act of showing respect didn't have to be based completely on merit? What if we could respect people simply by virtue of their God-given humanity? Is it possible to disagree with someone, to not allow them to bully or control us, to not turn a blind eye to their imperfections, and yet still show them this kind of respect? Every feed on your phone and every story on your TV shouts, "No!' But what if God's way says, "Yes!"? In today's world, this would be truly rebellious. This would make us countercultural.

No other relationship brings us more face-to-face with another person's clear and evident faults than marriage. So choosing kindness and respect for each other in marriage is nothing less than a rebellious act that produces revolutionary repercussions.

POWER BALANCES AND BLAME

I'm not letting anyone off the hook—not in marriage or in the world around us—by talking about respect. The apostle Paul didn't either. He told Titus, a young leader, "In everything set them an example by doing what is good. In your teaching show integrity, seriousness and soundness of speech that cannot be condemned, so that those who oppose you may be ashamed because they have nothing bad to say about us" (Titus 2:7–8). Paul also wrote to the Philippians about similar expectations, not just for leaders, but for anyone who followed Christ. Unapologetically, he wrote, "Let your gentle spirit [your graciousness, unselfishness, mercy, tolerance, and patience] be known to all people. The Lord is near" (Philippians 4:5 AMP).

Some Christians today claim to take God's commandments literally, but for some reason, they dismiss or reframe this very direct *command* to be gracious, tolerant, patient, and gentle to "all people"—even the ones we disagree with. They instead embrace bitter thoughts, petty rivalries, and even childish name-calling. It's all too easy to find ways to put such command from Scripture into any mental category one can think of besides immediate and unconditional obedience.

I certainly did this in my marriage. I was mostly aligned with the gracious, tolerant, patient stuff toward anyone I met at church, in the grocery store, or out on the street. To strangers, I not only looked the part but also genuinely did a decent job of keeping this commandment. But I hadn't yet come to the realization of what "all people" meant. There were some people—namely, one in particular who lived in my house and shared a last name with me—toward whom I had become disrespectful on a regular basis.

Our friends were coming to town in a few days to go to the Detroit Lions football game. We were excited for them to experience game day with their whole family. Everything was arranged—dinner at our house with all the kids, a great hotel at which we had made reservations months before, and tickets for great seats that Dave had gotten from some of the football players who attended our Lions Bible study.

Dave told me he was going to call the hotel to make sure the rooms were next to each other since our friends had a big family. I could hear him in his office, his voice radiating concern. I stepped into the doorway to see what was up. Our eyes met, and I could see the frustration on his face.

"Yes, I made the reservations months ago. I'm positive. How could you not have the reservation?"

He was calm, kind, and cool, which was typical of Dave.

I could tell he was frustrated but he was incredibly patient with the person on the other end of the phone.

"Well, can I reserve two rooms for those same dates if you can't find my reservation? Sold out? You have nothing available? Yes, I know this is a big game and every hotel is probably booked. That's why I called months ago."

I took another step into the room and waved at Dave to get his attention. "Give me the phone," I whispered emphatically. He turned his back on me, ignoring my plea and kept talking to the person on the phone.

I maneuvered my way around him so he could see me. He again walked away, ignoring me. Now I was motioning with my hand as I said in a loud voice, "Give me the phone!"

Why did I want the phone? Because I could get things done. That's who I am. I'm a closer! Dave was being so nice that he wasn't getting the point across about how important this was and how *they* were in the wrong. I could do a much better job of making that happen.

Looking back, I'm appalled at my arrogance.

I pestered Dave several more times, following him around the house, badgering him to give me the phone. Finally, he looked at me in total exasperation and disgust, threw the phone on the floor, and marched away, shouting, "Why don't you just cut 'it' off, Ann!"

I was stunned by his reaction, which was nothing like that of the chill guy I had married. I pridefully picked up the phone, thinking, *Well, I'll show him how to get things done.*

Guess what? I was no more successful than Dave at nabbing those rooms.

Conviction and shame flooded every part of me as I hung

up the phone. I had emasculated my husband—and to what gain? Even if I had been able to convince the hotel to give us the rooms, was it worth the cost of making my husband feel like the biggest loser of a man?

I knew I needed to change. But first I needed to apologize.

To be clear, my words to Dave were rarely blatantly attacking or demeaning. But remember the Arbinger research about how people will always immediately recognize your "way of being" toward them? This phenomenon is true, and Dave's valid feelings about being booed are exhibit A. He felt disrespected, not just because of his own insecurity, but because I was absolutely not respecting him in my mind, especially when he let me down. My way of being and words to him were much more powerful elements of my marriage than I realized. I may have felt like a forgotten nobody raising three little boys while my husband was off taking the world by storm, but the truth is, I was a real influencer. I just didn't know it or appreciate it, which kept me from appreciating Dave.

Since we have such power as women to affect and influence our men, how should we use it? That is, where does our real power lie? One day, I was hanging out and chatting with a group of female friends when one of them said with a mischievous grin in a way I've never forgotten: "Let's just be honest. We can make our husbands do anything we want." Everyone agreed because everyone knew she was right. When we were honest with one another, we all knew we had the power to spin, tweak, withdraw, withhold, blow up, or otherwise manipulate to get from our men whatever we wanted. But just because we *can* wield our wife power in such ways, does that mean we *should*?

In our culture, everything in marriage is a fifty-fifty split. There is some truth to this in that we should be equally yoked in partnership together—and yes, we should also share the tasks of running a home and family equally. But the world's definition of fifty-fifty takes it further. The idea is that if we perceive our husbands to be on the wrong end of a thirty-five/sixty-five split, the obvious injustice warrants our disrespect or manipulation. We are free to use our power in any way we deem necessary to restore the fifty-fifty balance or, worse, tip it in our favor.

But what is God's design for women, who are obviously such powerful image bearers of his divine nature? Is it a perfect balance of power and blame between husband and wife? These questions are important because unless we ask them, we may not know that we're already living in step with the way the world answers them. We can intentionally choose God's design, or we can unintentionally fall into the culture's demise.

I believe a majority of the conflict that takes place in marriage is comparison based—who has it the hardest, or who is doing more? I used to think, *Dave is not giving 50 percent. He's giving more like 30. Why should I do my part if he's not doing his?* And as we've learned from the power of negative thought patterns, I eventually convinced myself that he was doing *nothing.* In my mind, I would completely remove his value from the equation. I would falsely believe I was doing 100 percent, which inadvertently made everything in our marriage 100 percent about *me.* I felt like I had to hold all the power so I could use it to get what I needed—because Dave was never going to be able to give me what I needed.

Power is like plutonium. It is not inherently good or bad.

It can literally be used to provide energy to a whole city, or it can be used to destroy a whole city. It can build something up, or it can blow something up. How power is used determines its value. Proverbs 14:1 reads, "The wise woman builds her house, but with her own hands the foolish one tears hers down." As wives, we are either building something or tearing something down, but how? Are we using our power to give energy—to build our families up? Or are we blowing things up on a regular basis?

For years, I was the one blowing things up. When Dave came through our front door, I would use my power to make him feel guilty or like a failure, which was ultimately destroying him rather than infusing him with kindness and respect so he could get the energy he needed. In my scarcity mindset, he wasn't giving me what I needed, so I wasn't going to give him what he needed. This common thought process in marriage stems from the idea of a fifty-fifty balance of personal responsibility and personal justice. We don't set out to think this way, but we are slowly lulled into it by the strivings and stresses of sharing a life and a family day after day, year after year. The heavy weight of repetitiveness digs deep new neurological pathways in our minds.

The thing is, though, no one will ever be able to fully satisfy all the requirements of what even their side of the 50 percent supposedly demands in order to create an equilibrium of justice for each partner. In our first book, *Vertical Marriage*, we talked about the horizontal lines between wives and husbands that are limited in their scope. The horizontal can never rise above a certain plane. It can only keep going left or right. There must be a third and very different line, a vertical line that isn't confined to our finite lefts and rights. We engage the vertical because we learn (perhaps the hard way) that we can never gain from another horizontal human what only a vertical God can provide.

We can only break free from the personal judgment way of life when we stop thinking our power in marriage is supposed to be used to equalize our horizontally shared lives so that they remain fair for everyone. Again, I'm not condoning any partner in marriage neglecting to show up and do their part, because obviously they should. If your mind is like mine, it tends to look for ways to dismiss certain principles by finding their exceptions in the extremes.

But the truth is, even in good relationships, marriage is not always balanced or fair. It just isn't. One partner will be weaker in certain areas or even in certain seasons, while another will be stronger. We should strive, not to equalize our responsibilities and privileges, but to recognize each other's weaknesses and choose to love and respect the other despite them. The beautiful unfairness of grace shows us that while our weaknesses may not be equal, they render each of us equally in need of God's strength. When we stop using our husband's weaknesses as excuses to misuse the power God has given us, we can break free from the cycles we're in. It is only outside of a human definition of flourishing that we can truly flourish in our marriage. After all, marriage is not a human idea.

In your vertical relationship with God, there is no fifty-fifty. He is the full 100 percent of everything you need to become the person you were created to be, married or otherwise. Achieving a perfect balance of fairness or personal justice in your marriage won't fill up everything that is lacking within you. As much as we talked about positive illusion in the last chapters, demanding personal justice as a path to inner completion is a negative illusion. As Scripture tells us, "So you also are complete through your union with Christ, who is the head over every ruler and authority (Colossians 2:10 NLT). The head is higher than the body, vertically above it, yet connected to it and directing it toward that which brings and sustains life.

Because we are complete in Christ, we are free to use our power for others instead of using it to fight and manipulate for ourselves, attempting to preserve whatever we think we deserve that is being withheld from us. We will rest with confidence in our relationship with Jesus. After all, "No good thing does he withhold from those whose walk is blameless" (Psalm 84:11). The only way we can be blameless is to humbly receive from Jesus the highest justification that exists only because he took the blame for us at the cross. Now that we are proclaimed blameless by his work and not our own, we are free to trust in his character, which proves once and for all that he is not trying to withhold any good thing from us.

With that truth in mind, we can break free from the scarcity mindset that led us to withhold good things from our husbands because we believed good things were being withheld from us. By God's grace, our husbands can do the same.

REBELS, RESPECT, AND REVERENCE

Power reaches its highest good when it is either given up or used for the good of others. No one was more powerful than Jesus Christ, and yet his deepest might was revealed when he laid down what everyone around him *thought* was his real power. He could heal, read people's thoughts, disappear into a crowd, multiply bread and fish for thousands, walk on water, and a hundred other "supernatural" things that, to this day, would blow anyone's mind who witnessed them. Jesus' power was obvious, even to those who didn't believe in him.

But in Philippians 2:5–8 (NLT), Paul points to the most potent element of Christ's power: "You must have the same attitude that Christ Jesus had. Though he was God, he did not think of equality with God as something to cling to. Instead, he gave up his divine privileges; he took the humble position of a slave and was born as a human being. When he appeared in human form, he humbled himself in obedience to God and died a criminal's death on a cross." Jesus gave up divine privileges he didn't have to give up. He left a magnificent heavenly home he didn't have to leave. He died a death he didn't have to die so that we wouldn't have to die the same death. He willingly took on sin and degradation, separated from the Father, for our sakes.

Giving up our privileges for someone else is a foreign concept to most people today. After all, we are told to scrape and claw to get everything that's ours—because no one else is going to take care of us. But Jesus rebelled against the ways of this world by giving up the rights he could have demanded. He went where he invites us to go—into a life where we trust that the Father will take care of us. Jesus' way released power for the benefit of more people. His way will do the same for us.

The next verses reveal the ultimate outcome for Jesus after he forfeited his ultimate privileges: "Therefore God exalted him to the highest place and gave him the name that is above every name, that at the name of Jesus every knee should bow, in heaven and on earth and under the earth, and every tongue acknowledge that Jesus Christ is Lord, to the glory of God the Father" (Philippians 2:9–11). Jesus' highest exaltation was the direct result of his basest humility. He was lifted up because he let himself be brought low and trusted that his highest good came from his trustworthy Father. He rebelled against the world's ways in order to save the world from its ways. Giving respect to our husbands and families is one of the highest forms of effective rebellion for us wives.*

Ephesians 5 is the biblical epicenter of the conversations swirling around respect in marriage: "However, each one of you also must love his wife as he loves himself, and the wife must respect her husband" (Ephesians 5:33). The apostle Paul is not saying that women should respect their husbands but don't have to love them as well. Nor does it mean that husbands must only love their wives but not respect them. I'm no scholar, but I think the differences in love and respect, as used in these verses, are more about what most deeply speaks to the inner souls of women and men, respectively. Both need love and respect, but each will generally seek these out differently.

When I first began working on these issues, I remember asking Dave if he knew that I loved him. Unequivocally, he said, "Yes." But then I asked if he thought I respected him. "Hmm, sometimes," he sheepishly answered.

"Which would you prefer?" I asked, interested in his answer.

---

*Yes, our husbands should respect us as well. Let me remind you that everything in this book about a wife's treatment of her husband could just as well be written about a husband's treatment of his wife. Any differences are more about context than substance. But this book is for you—for women. Perhaps Dave will write a book just for men.

"Both, but respect feels very affirming and powerful to me, like something I need in my soul from you."

Interesting, isn't it? What a great question to ask your spouse. I know I definitely want Dave to respect me. Who doesn't want that? Sometimes, depending on what we're doing, I might long for respect more than love. For example, I want his respect for me as an author and communicator. But speaking in generalizations, I would typically prefer feeling loved in our day-in and day-out encounters. Every couple is different, but the hope is that you will become an expert on your own spouse and marriage.

If I want to speak life to Dave, I need to learn how to speak to him in a way that communicates my respect for him, which can feel rebellious these days. Obviously, I also want to be an expert on how to love Dave as well. Love and respect go hand in hand.

So if we set out to rebel by showing respect, what does it entail? Does it mean we say, "Yes, sir," and "No, sir"? I can assure you this most certainly does *not* happen in the Wilson home. Perhaps a better path to understanding respect is to look more deeply at the verse in question. The Amplified Bible "amplifies" the English translations of single words or phrases by adding brackets with expanded definitions of the words from the original languages. This approach can be helpful for this sometimes hotly debated verse:

However, each man among you [without exception] is to love his wife as his very own self [with behavior worthy of respect and esteem, always seeking the best for her with an attitude of lovingkindness], and the wife [must see to it] that she respects and delights in her husband [that she notices him and prefers him and treats him with loving concern, treasuring him, honoring him, and holding him dear]. (Ephesians 5:33 AMP).

I kind of resent the way this verse spells it out, but I love it too. I know that the resentment comes from my old wounds of watching my mom get taken advantage of. To be honest, depending on one's past, this verse can be activating in hard ways. At the time of this writing, even with all the work I've done in these areas, I still have so much further to go in pursuing health in my inner emotional self. The learning and the leaning on Jesus never end.

But when it comes to Ephesians 5, this glimpse into the original meaning of these words certainly limits any extreme interpretations—such as, that men only want respect and women only want love. Since we're women, let's focus on our part because it shows us what respect for our husbands should look like. God wants us to delight in our husbands—meaning, we are meant to experience joy when we think or talk about him. When a wife who delights in her husband shows him respect, she doesn't bow down to him or lose her own identity in his overlordship. No. Instead, she notices him. She prefers him (remember, he prefers her as well). She treats him with loving concern. She treasures him. She honors him. She holds him dear.

As always, Scripture says it best. You could close this book and pray that God will help you do these things, and you will experience incredible changes in yourself and your marriage. (But please don't close the book yet because we still have so much to talk about! Who gave you such a crazy idea in the first place?)

I know this can be super hard to read, especially if things aren't going well in your marriage. This idea of treasuring or holding your husband dear feels like something for an alien on another planet, not someone in your marriage. I encourage you to return to the ideas we discussed in previous chapters about the power of positive and negative thought patterns. But apart from what you can do in your own mind, you may be in a situation where your husband does not treasure and hold you dear, let alone lay down his life for you. So it makes sense that you have no idea how to show him respect, though he needs it from you.

Another verse from Ephesians 5 may help, though maybe not at first glance: "Submit to one another out of reverence for Christ" (Ephesians 5:21). I get it. People get rightfully a little shifty when someone uses the *s*-word in a religious way. Certainly, many men over the centuries have overlooked the *without exception* part of loving their wives as their selves *with behavior worthy of respect and esteem, always seeking the best for her with an attitude of lovingkindness* (v. 33 AMP). They have polluted the idea of submission for selfish gain. They have not used their God-given power for the benefit of others, but rather for themselves and the systems they are propping up.

But Ephesians 5:21 doesn't have to sound screwy. As the verse that leads into the debated sections on marriage and the varying roles of wives and husbands, this verse reveals God's heart for the issue as a whole. To get lost in the weeds of controversy would mean ignoring this part of the passage, which seems pretty cut-and-dried. Submission is supposed to be *mutual* between husbands and wives, not just something that one does for the other. Even if we want to focus the discussion on the leadership role of the husband, which I am not arguing against, the Bible is clear that real leadership looks like humility and laying down one's own privileges and desires for the sake of someone else (see the previous paragraphs on Ephesians 2:5–8).

Maybe you're thinking, *That's all well and good, Ann, but my husband will never submit to me in any form or fashion. How am I supposed to show him that kind of respect when I am constantly being disrespected?*

First, I hear you, and I pray that God works in your marriage and in your husband's hardened heart. This is such a difficult reality for so many women. I'm cheering for you, and I know God is doing the same! Let me reiterate that submission is not a license for abuse of any kind. A great therapist, biblical counselor, pastor, or godly friend is especially important in such situations, so don't go it alone or remain isolated.

Second, this verse itself contains a clue that may bring you comfort and give you context for trying out this rightly defined submission. For what reason are each of us supposed to submit to the other? Because the other is doing their 50 percent? No. We submit not out of reverence for the other person, but "out of reverence for Christ" (Ephesians 5:21). Think vertically on this one. Respect is what we can give our husbands only when reverence is what we're giving our Savior.

Reverence for Christ doesn't mean being pious or perfect in your prayers and Bible reading. It doesn't mean never getting angry or never yelling at your husband. It doesn't mean you will "feel" some faith-induced euphoria on a daily basis. Trust me, there are times you will feel only the negative—or nothing at all.

Reverence for God isn't about any of that. It doesn't require you to be a fixture of goodness or patience. God is the fixture in your marriage, the point of origin of any love, joy, peace—that is, any goodness—you may experience. You don't go scrape up some goodness so you can approach a holy God. You offer him reverence when you come as you are—day after day, unworthy moment after unworthy moment, doubt after doubt—trusting that goodness only comes from him. Goodness can't begin with us, so we can take a breath of relief as we "come boldly to the throne of our gracious God. There we will receive his mercy, and we will find grace to help us when we need it most" (Hebrews 4:16 NLT).

God won't change his mind about you just because your mind and thoughts are constantly changing. Reverence for him means trusting in and receiving his love for you over and over again, even when you feel like you don't deserve it or that God isn't making things any easier for you. Reverence is returning, even if you've fallen down a million times. Return! Be a rebel who keeps rising from the ashes to face the next challenge, no matter how many times you've been knocked down. Don't give up, because I promise Jesus cannot give up on you. "For great is his love toward us, and the faithfulness of the Lord endures forever" (Psalm 117:2).

Forever means an eternity of faithfulness. And even when you feel so weak and doubtful, it doesn't diminish God's eternal faithfulness because even "if we are faithless, he remains faithful, for he *cannot* disown himself" (2 Timothy 2:13, emphasis mine). When you are his, he is with you every step of the way, seeing your tears, feeling your disappointment, understanding your anger and loneliness. He is the One I lean on every single day because I cannot do any of this without his power and grace.

You can show your husband a rightly defined, biblically informed level of respect, yes, maybe in spite of him, because your deepest reverence is already going to the One you can trust the most. Your man may have lied or changed his mind over the years, but I have good news: "God is not a man, that He should lie, nor a son of man, that He should repent [that is, change His mind]. Has He said, and will He not do it? Or has He spoken and will He not make it good and fulfill it?" (Numbers 23:19 AMP; this bracketed aside is mine and not a part of the Amplified Bible's normal brackets).

The rebellion of respect is something we can do, not because our husbands are fully deserving, but because we are fully devoted to God and his ways, trusting that he will do what only he can do, which frees us to do what we could never do before—and do it with joy! Remember when I said this is not for the faint of heart? This is where we get real in our walk with God. When we know him as a good and loving Father, we can trust him. I have to keep myself constantly in God's Word to remember and remind myself that I can trust him because he loves me and gave his life for me.

He loves you too! Do you believe it?

DAVE'S REFLECTION

I love Ann's take on kindness and respect and how they are ways to rebel against the current culture. Ann has hinted at how strong she is as a person, but now that I have the visual microphone for a second, I can say what she would never say about herself. Ann is not just strong; she's a beast! A beautiful beast, obviously. I just mean that her strength and abilities are off the charts.

So when it comes to someone as capable as Ann, I can understand why respecting someone who is disappointing her would be difficult. In our younger years, there were so many things both of us still had to learn. Of course, she was the one doing the lioness's share of work at home all day long with our kids. It wasn't fair—and as Ann said, marriage often isn't. But regardless, she was also still hurting me because I often felt like she did not honor me as a person and as a man.

Then she turned her strength into a beautifully rebellious act! I kid you not when I say that feeling genuine respect, honor, and affirmation from the person I love the most in this world changed my life.

Many authors, including us, say that giving love and respect is like inflating our hearts with life. I've seen it in Ann. It helps her breathe and survive because these are her greatest needs. Sadly, I've seen that look on Ann's face when I haven't been filling her heart with love and respect—especially tender love. It's as though she has lost her joy as her heart is weakened by a lack of what brings her life.

The man also needs his heart to be inflated with love and

respect. For me, respect is like the oxygen my heart needs to beat on a regular basis. Ann can willfully stop this flow of respect. And yes, it's true that we men certainly don't always deserve it. The good news is that she can also turn up that flow to high speed by her belief in me, which is like filling my heart with oxygenated blood, which brings life to my whole body.

I remember one time we were sitting down at the dinner table with the kids. Ann had been reading about my need for respect and decided to practice right then and there. Just before we were about to pray, Ann said, "Hey, boys, before we eat, I just want to say, 'Dave, thank you for being the provider in our family. Thank you for supplying all this food on our table and for our house.'"

None of us had ever heard her speak like that before. I was floored, and so were the boys. Ann could tell we weren't sure what to say, so she broke the awkward silence, "Seriously, you guys need to know that your dad is amazing."

I think my chest almost burst right out of my shirt at that very moment. I can't overstate how those words impacted me. Now, I could see a book on the hutch about loving and respecting one's spouse, so I figured out pretty quickly that she was probably doing what the book had told her to do. But you know what, I didn't even care. I could tell that she really meant what she said. And even if someone had to coach her into saying it, it felt so good. I thought, *Ann thinks I'm the man!*

I think she caught on to the power of her good rebellion pretty quickly after that. She figured out that it's not particularly difficult to verbally affirm me with words such as, "Thank you"; "I'm proud of you"; and "I believe in you." As Ann said, there are always exceptions, but in my nearly forty years of ministry, I've never met a husband who doesn't want to hear these things from his wife.

If you are a husband reading this, let me say this: We need to live in a way that will garner respect and belief from our wives. When we act in unrespectable ways, it is extremely difficult for our wives to respect us. How we live matters, and a man who lives in a respectable way will find respect and belief coming back to him.

I know you wives want to hear the same thing from your husband. We are called by God to give love and respect back to you. But let me remind you, your affirming words of belief truly do help him become the man you thought you married.

CHAPTER 6

GOING BACK TO GO FORWARD

"So if the Son sets you free, you will be free indeed."

JOHN 8:36

All this talk of rebellion sounds great, doesn't it? It makes me want to strap on some serious (yet stylish) armor, mount a colorful warhorse, and ride headlong into the perils of battle—Wonder Woman style! That's exactly how you feel too, right?

Okay, so maybe you're not ready to become the female William Wallace, but I do hope that the reverse realities of God's ways are illuminating new rooms in your soul, rooms that may have been closed off for quite some time. In chapter 4, I shared briefly about my upbringing and how it affected me. Here I want to expand on that part of my story. In doing so, my hope is that you will see the benefits and find the courage to see the ways your past is shaping your present, including your view of yourself and your husband.

I also hope to help you learn to recognize *in the moment* those patterns of thought and communication that can so easily derail us, causing us to miss our chance to rebel against the wrong ways. If we can wake up in these very moments and take steps toward reactions different from the ones we've always chosen, we can begin to write a new story for ourselves and our marriages. However, if we don't learn to deal with our origin stories, they will keep dealing with us.

"NOW IS NOT THE TIME, ANN"

Most marriages have a carousel issue that continues to cycle through over and over again, just minus the carnival music and the corn dogs. For years, almost every one of our fights had cyclical themes. His was about insecurity; mine was about not being a priority for him. To me, everything else in Dave's life was more important than I was. My inner narratives were tired and predictable, yet they wouldn't back down: *He doesn't see me. He doesn't hear me. He doesn't value me. He doesn't know me.* And the thing was, Dave could tell me—and at times even show me—that these inner messages were mine, not his. But even that didn't make them go away.

I wish I could tell you that eventually they completely went away. Truth is, they have certainly gotten better, but I can still become triggered, which can be discouraging. Why? Because they are not coming out of nowhere. Just as I talked about my words in chapter 2, these particular inner narratives and messages are attached to something inside me that reaches deeper than I can see from the surface. Yes, I have spent more than thirty years talking and writing about healthy marriages, but this doesn't mean all of my own issues have been completely resolved. Though healing can come in single moments of repentance and breakthrough, it is also an ongoing path, not an instant arrival. We may have experienced some healing, but God's goal is that we keep experiencing it deeper and deeper each passing day.

To that end, about four years ago, I went to an excellent Christian therapist for an intensive, which means we spent an entire day together digging deep into my past. Dave went too. I didn't go because my faith in God wasn't working. It is all too easy for those of us whose lives are informed by faith and religion to shy away from the beautiful diversity found in a wide range of tools God can use to shape us. I'll talk more about this later in the chapter, but just know that going to a therapist didn't mean that prayer, Bible reading, church, and community had failed me; it just meant that some closed-off areas of my heart were being discovered—rooms that had remained out of sight and out of mind for years. I needed additional methods to invite God's healing into these places. Therapy became a useful tool, helping to confirm many things God had already been revealing, as well as uncovering new ones.

My therapist began by asking me about my family of origin. Funny how our families can be so familiar to us, yet so much can be subtly hidden in the plain sight of familiarity. We assume we know everything about the ways we have been affected by the people we grew up with—after all, we spent day after day, year after year with them. But just because we know *what once happened* to us doesn't necessarily mean we know *all that is still happening* as a result. No, it isn't all trauma, and no, it isn't all negative—though certainly some of it is both.

Over the years of words, experiences, and formative development, the values and dynamics of our family seep into our subconscious. They become second nature to us—one of the main lenses through which we view the world around us. But just as if you forgot to take off your sunglasses as dusk begins to descend, you may not realize that your shaded lenses are making everything else appear much darker than it really is. Recognizing the lens through which you see life is harder than you think—after all, you've only looked *through* it your whole life. This is why stopping to look *at it* requires a new level of self-awareness. If you want to think about things differently, you must adopt a new way of thinking—a different lens.

As I told my story, the therapist wrote some of my words on a whiteboard. The facts of my childhood experiences began rising to the surface as impressions and beliefs I never knew I had. "I'm the youngest of four. My parents were great people. They were amazing in so many ways and did their best." A long pause. "But they were busy. As the youngest, I came to understand that when you have three older siblings, you're not always going to be the priority."

I proceeded to tell him a story that was obviously a core memory for me. I was in third grade, and I came home from school with what I thought was an amazing playground story I couldn't wait to tell. When we all sat down at the dinner table, I couldn't hold it in any longer. I began blabbering about my playground adventures. Dad was sitting right beside me.

He put his hand on my arm and said, "Ann, now is not the time for your stories."

"What do you mean?" I asked innocently.

"Well, this is your brother's time. Jim is the oldest, so this is his time to share with the family."

I was distraught. If I had to wait for everyone who was older than me to say everything they wanted to say, I'd never get to tell anyone what was important in my life. What's more, it was common for the older kids to leave the table when they were finished to run off to their next practice, date, or whatever else they had to do. "But, Dad," I pleaded, "by the time I get to talk, nobody will be here but you and Mom."

Despite my protests, it was what it was. My older brother told his latest baseball story. Everyone else told theirs. Everyone left the table. I sat in silence alone. No one, it seemed, even cared about the story I wanted to tell. I was left to feel I was not a priority. Everyone else was more important. Even sports were more important. I simply wasn't as important.

At this point in my life, having raised three kids, I get it. My parents were pre-mourning the loss of their oldest son, who would soon be leaving for college. They had a lot going on, and I know they loved me dearly. They didn't mean to hurt me. I know my kids have their own stories of ways I have failed them. None of us make it through parenting without hurting our kids. No individual is one-dimensional. We are more complex than that. This complexity is why it's hard to balance the truth that my parents were great people with the fact that I often didn't receive as much attention as my siblings.

My parents loved me, but they had no idea how to show it. Yes, it was a different time when girls and boys were treated much differently than today. That was the reality, yet it is not a valid excuse. And it hurt me deeply. No matter how it happened or whether they had the best of intentions, I rarely felt seen or heard. When this is your perceived reality, you set out to change it. I remember pointing out to my dad that my brothers weren't the only good athletes. I was a good one too. Even so, I don't remember my dad coming to even one of my gymnastics meets. After all my siblings had graduated and left home, he came to one of my track meets, but his presence made me so nervous that it didn't turn out to be a good thing.

As I told these stories and saw their visual elements written on the whiteboard by the therapist, I realized I had lived my life thinking that my past was what it was. Yet it was becoming more apparent with each stroke of his dry erase marker, my past wasn't completely in the past tense—that is, it also *still* is what it is. No, we are not solely shaped by what happens to us. Yes, we have personalities apart from our experiences—our wiring if you will. We also have choices about how we react to the good and bad in our lives, which is why different people respond to similar trauma in very different ways.

My personality and choices led me to work harder so that I would always be the best. After all, I was raised to believe that second place is a loser's prize. I became the one who shows up—a high-level performer, which again translated into unreasonable expectations in my marriage that Dave should also perform at a high level. I didn't just want to be best individual in the world; I wanted our marriage to be the best in the world too.

What could go wrong?

But there were deeper things at play than just showing up

as the best. My parents truly were wonderful in so many ways, but saying, "I love you," was not something they did. They also rarely hugged us. Fast-forward to my entrance into marriage, and you find a young woman who didn't even know she was about to require of her new husband *everything* she didn't get as a kid. When we were dating, just the fact that Dave noticed me and hugged me was a huge deal—bigger than I realized at the time.

But as we all know, dating and marriage are two completely different animals. I subconsciously believed that marriage would fill the emotional crater left over from my childhood. I would finally be seen enough. Hugged enough. Told "I love you" enough. Noticed enough. My opinions would matter enough to be listened to. I would be enough—well, as long as Dave did enough of these things enough of the time. Neither of us knew exactly how much my origin story had deeply affected my expectations of him early in our marriage. Back then, I didn't realize that even if he did each of these things to a tee, the crater inside me would be far from filled. No matter what, nothing would be enough.

STAGES

I wish somebody had told me when I was younger that if something keeps popping up as a problem in my present, it's probably from my past. It may feel like it's way back there somewhere, but we each carry life's collective experiences forward to the next season or stage of life—like a knapsack on our journey. This isn't all bad. It's actually one of the ways we grow and mature. But when it comes to negative experiences, this pack can get pretty heavy.

If you're a person of faith, all this talk about the past affecting the present may seem confusing or contradictory to what you've been taught in Christian circles. As someone who pastored a local church with my husband for more than thirty years, I am fully aware of the ideas and movements that come and go in the religious world. In some of these circles, the past has been taught as something to be completely forgotten, to be put behind us. After all, Scripture says, "No, dear brothers and sisters, I have not achieved it, but I focus on this one thing: *Forgetting the past* and looking forward to what lies ahead" (Philippians 3:13 NLT, emphasis mine). If we're supposed to forget the past, why are we talking about therapy and dredging up old issues?

It would be easy to take one isolated verse and build around it, but it's a better practice to let this verse dwell in the wider context of Scripture as a whole. It is doubtful that Paul meant "never think of the past," since he himself spoke often of his own past and his history with his readers. He even references past difficulties: "Surely you remember that I was sick when I first brought you the Good News" (Galatians 4:13 NLT), and "Don't forget that you Gentiles used to be outsiders" (Ephesians 2:11 NLT).

In fact, when it comes to moving forward in his divine mission, Paul is continually looking back in remembrance, even of his own failures. In Philippians 3, he goes into great detail about the ways he had kept the Jewish law as a younger man, which led him to persecute Christians. This couldn't have been an easy part of his life to remember, but it informed his life and testimony in the present. It made him all the more humble and grateful for where he was in the present, focused on what he should be doing now in light of what he did then.

Paul didn't forget his past, but he did put it into proper perspective, which kept him from being controlled by it. "I once thought these things were valuable," he wrote, "but now I consider them worthless because of what Christ has done" (Philippians 3:7 NLT). To be clear, the memories themselves weren't worthless or he wouldn't have constantly referenced them. It was the former way of thinking and living that was now worthless to him in his new life in Christ.

Dave and I were young zealous believers when we got married. We thought we were completely leaving the past behind—after all, why drum up old pain when we had finally moved on? There was plenty of well-meaning religious language to support this viewpoint. Since we were free in Christ, we were exempt from carrying our own origin stories forward into the next chapter. The generational curses had been broken. We were more than conquerors.

Unknowingly, however, we used the pursuit of spiritual health as a smoke screen for our emotional health. In fact, terms like "emotional health" were rarely used in the 1990s when we were shepherding a young and growing church. And if they were, they were considered taboo. The beef that many religious circles had with the very idea of emotional health was simple: If we have the grace of Jesus, the love of God, and the power and fellowship of the Holy Spirit, we should be completely healed in all areas of life, including our mental and emotional health. Dave and I thought we'd have a great marriage because of the same things. Jesus had died for us. What else could we need?

What we failed to realize was that doing the work of seeking deeper emotional health does not counteract or deny the work of Jesus in our lives. On the contrary, the work of Jesus is ongoing and reaches into all areas of our lives, including our emotional health. Scripture confirms this continuing work: "For the word of God is alive and active. Sharper than any double-edged sword, it penetrates even to dividing soul and spirit, joints and marrow; it judges *the thoughts and attitudes of the heart*" (Hebrews 4:12, emphasis mine).

Note that God's work in us doesn't stop at "religious things," such as our ability to resist sins, share our faith, read our Bibles, and pray regularly. The words in this verse are much more surgical and intimate. God delves far past our present behaviors. His grace and truth, which are the essences of his Word (John 1:14), address those events and issues in our lives that have sunk deep into our bones—so deep that we often don't even know they're there. God is active in these deeper places, revealing the hidden thoughts and attitudes of our hearts—that is, our inner or emotional selves.

When we come to know Christ, we receive a real and total salvation. We move from death to life. In C. S. Lewis's masterpiece *The Lion, the Witch, and the Wardrobe*, the lion Aslan is killed by the White Witch. All hope is lost for a land that is stuck in eternal winter. But when Aslan rises from the dead, everything changes. However, it doesn't change in an instant. The snow and ice begin to melt, and nothing can stop them from disappearing someday, but it doesn't happen immediately. The winter keeps melting away, but some ice remains.

Such is our life in Christ. The death inside us has been reversed and we are alive, but as long as we have life in this world, snow and ice remain that will someday melt away for good. Sin. Struggle. Security issues. Yet we keep growing. Maturing. Becoming who will we someday be in all our fullness. This both instantaneous and progressive nature of our salvation is not less miraculous than the instantaneous version alone, but more! Why? Because even though there is still ice to be melted, we get to keep living in this adventure with "Aslan," our Savior. We are chosen characters in a story Christ is writing across the pages of history and eternity.

When Dave and I were young, we had different ideas. We thought that being married Christian adults meant we would instantly become mature and healed in most of the ways that mattered in life. Boy, were we in for a surprise! We found out that, yes, Christ did finish the work of redemption at the cross, initiating the reversal of the eternal winter of sin and death in this world. But there is more to our healing than what happens when we "get saved" in the here and now. Some of God's best work happens as he keeps healing us later on. All of us. Mind. Body. Soul. Spirit.

Our emotional selves are not excluded from all that God wants to heal. It all counts, and all of it is open to God's inner work. But if we think there is some way to silo our spiritual selves away from our emotional selves, we are sorely mistaken. As Pete Scazzero says, "It's impossible to be spiritually mature while remaining emotionally immature."[1] And there is no path to emotional maturity that doesn't acknowledge the various events and stages that have led us to this point. Yes, Paul was right about not letting those things hold us back from moving forward, but I don't think he meant that the past should never be remembered. We can't move forward without looking back.

Remember when we started this journey back in chapter 1? It was like we were standing on the shore, looking out and focusing on our words. Make no mistake: now we are way out in the deep. Our emotional stories and health are what cause us to think and speak in the way we do, in marriage or otherwise. This is where the waves begin that eventually hit the shoreline, sometimes as a tidal wave of anger or resentment. Just as we can't stop a wave from the shore, we can't just decide to start speaking differently while we leave our thoughts and emotions as they were. To do so would not only be inauthentic, but also ineffective. You can only fake your words for so long before what really lies beneath comes bubbling to the surface, even if only in other ways like passive-aggressiveness, control, and lying.

In a worst-case scenario that is tragically not uncommon, some husbands and wives say the right things at home, but keep their emotional selves so distant and unaddressed for so long that they eventually drift into infidelity. No one just jumps into bed with a stranger one day. There is a process of denying one thing—your own emotional health—that eventually makes room for another thing. It is a long pathway of burying and hiding inner pain and patterns over time, leading people to do things they never thought they would do way back when they stood at an altar and genuinely vowed, "Till death do us part." When we refuse to do the work of looking at our past, even our past vows can become lost in the emotional tidal waves.

The work is never done. And these few pages are just the

introduction to a primer. But hopefully, at least when you now hear the words "doing the work of emotional health," you can rest assured that I'm not talking about work that bypasses the work of Jesus. Rather, this work opens up more areas of our lives to be affected and transformed by the work of Jesus. The work of changing lives is his alone to do. Trust me, I tried for a long time, but I ultimately and miserably failed at changing my inner self by my own means. Only Jesus brings life out of dead places. But just because Christ's work is the only kind that can change a heart doesn't mean there is no work for me to do as well.

If we can learn to make sense of our past events and stages of life, we will find that they no longer have to hold us captive. We can, in fact, be free! But if we don't take hold of this freedom, we will constantly think, speak, and act in certain ways that hurt ourselves and our marriages—and we won't even know why we keep doing it. We will be tempted to blame a situation on our husbands, blind to our own contributing patterns of negative thinking, speaking, and acting.

As I've said many times, this is *not* to say that your husband isn't at fault in his own ways. I repeat this not because you haven't heard it already, but because the repetition may keep you from falling back into whatever rut—that is, preexisting neural pathways—that compels you to only see the fault of another. Yes, everything in this book is equally true for men and should be equally applied to their thoughts, words, and behaviors. Remind yourself of this once again, because otherwise, you might become hesitant to look deeply within yourself or look back at your own story and patterns in every previous stage of your life's development. But the work is worth it!

CAGES

Yes, looking back can be painful, but trust me, it is much less painful than moving forward unhealed. There is so much to be gained when we let Jesus into the areas of our lives that have kept us captive to old and broken patterns of thinking. To illustrate this idea when I'm speaking, I sometimes crawl inside a dog cage (yes, I'm a very short person). I tell the audience that this is what it felt like when I was trapped inside the multitude of negative thoughts that were fueled by my own emotional story, the one that eventually led to unhealthy expectations of and reactions toward Dave. I haven't even mentioned the sexual abuse I experienced as a young girl that heaped shame and guilt on me—and though I don't have time to unpack that incident here, it undoubtedly played a huge role in what I was feeling. All of this reveals that, in actuality, the issues had as much to do with me as they did with Dave, if not more.

Inside that cage, I wasn't trapped by negative thoughts only about Dave but about myself as well. I was too often "in my own head." I was trapped by thoughts of shame. Failure. Insecurity. Inadequacy. Martyrdom. Anger. Unforgiveness. Comparison. Negative body image. Self-hate. And, believe it or not, so much more. Yet on the outside, I appeared happy and well put together.

One negative thought spawns another, like little gremlins in your head. This is not the life Jesus had in mind for us. Not in the least. He said, "I have come that they may have *life*, and have it to the *full*" (John 10:10, emphasis mine). *Life*. *Full*. These are the kinds of terms that describe Christ's true intentions toward us.

But we often quote the last part of John 10 without reading the beginning of the verse: "The thief comes *only* to *steal* and *kill* and *destroy*." *Steal. Kill. Destroy.* These are the kinds of terms that describe the thief of this world. But the most powerful word of all in this verse may be *only*. This is all he does, and he does nothing else.

The lies in our heads most certainly show up from the past and the pain that we have experienced, but let's not forget that there is an enemy of our soul, Satan, who takes advantage of every weakness and wound. He is a cowardly opportunist. A counterfeiter. This is all that he does. He longs to keep us caged in our past, whispering repeated lies in the hopes that we will never become the women, wives, and moms God intends us to be.

Back on the stage, I then tell the crowd what happened when Jesus came along. He kicked that cage door wide open! This is salvation. God sees us in our captivity, comes near to us, and opens the door. You're only a prisoner if there is no door or no door open through which you can exit. But once a door is open, you are free! Just ask anyone in prison who has had their prison door opened and have been told they are free to go. Even as they stand in their old cell, they are free!

We are free in Christ, but as I demonstrate in my illustration, sometimes we stay in our cages, even though the door is open. We don't stay because we want to. We stay because we haven't done the work to know what's going on inside ourselves so we can break free from our harmful patterns and walk freely into better places. After all, most any place is better than a dog's cage.

Crawling into a dog cage is difficult to do, even for short

people. But once you've sat all crowded in that cage for even fifteen minutes, crawling out is even harder. Your legs get stiff. Your back hurts. Your foot falls asleep. Moving out of that position will cause awkwardness and discomfort. It's no wonder that we often stay in the cage of our emotional wounds and negative patterns, even when the door to freedom is open. It takes discomfort and work to crawl through the door, but freedom lies on the other side. Emotionally, have you been in a cage of your own for years on end? What are the negative thoughts that continue to bombard you about yourself or your spouse? It's time to get free.

Jesus came to "proclaim freedom for the prisoners and recovery of sight for the blind, [and] to set the oppressed free" (Luke 4:18). His death and resurrection opened the door to our freedom—it remains as wide open as his tomb on the day the stone was rolled away. But now the question is, will we step out of our cages and walk in the newness of this freedom? Again, why wouldn't we? Leaving makes sense on paper, but the reason that most of us don't know how to walk into that freedom is that we're still all balled up in postures, positions, and patterns dictated by our past. We are free to go; we just don't know how.

This idea of being free versus walking in freedom or staying in freedom is scriptural. Paul tells us, "Since we live by the Spirit, let us keep in step with the Spirit" (Galatians 5:25). This statement demonstrates that it is possible to be made alive by something, yet not fully walk according to what made us alive. This doesn't mean we're not alive; it just means we aren't walking in a way that shows it. We're still in a cage— and that is not how we are intended to live. Paul continues,

"It is *for freedom* that Christ has set us free" (vs. 1a). In other words, Jesus opened the door with the intention that we would actually walk out into freedom. He didn't do it for show. He did it so we could actually live in the freedom he has granted, not just sit back and know that it exists. "Stand firm, then, and do not let yourselves be burdened again by a yoke of slavery" (vs. 1b). In other words, get out of the cage, stay out of the cage, and be sure not to get back into the cage.

The enemy wants us to get back into the cage—to return to our old emotional and communication patterns. It is tempting, not because it brought us freedom, but because it is familiar. This is why we must be willing to examine what events and patterns in our past have led us to such familiar words, thoughts and actions. Yes, we are free! But I've heard it said that the words your mind thinks become the house, or in our case, the cage, your heart lives in. This is why Christ implores us to stay free, which must mean that it is possible to be technically free, but to return to bondage in some areas of our lives.

We are about to explore some practical steps to stay out of the wrong mindset that leads to the wrong words and patterns of action. But for now, I offer one super simple and easy way to stay out of the cage: speak up when you feel yourself moving back toward that doggy door. This is called confession—and it's not just a "Get Out of Jail Free" card; it's also a "Stay Out of Jail and Stay Free" card. Doing it requires not only awareness of our patterns, but also a willing humility to speak up when we're tempted to return to the cage.

One day recently, I was in a meeting with a group of super-sharp friends. Each woman was very successful and influential in their own right. Suddenly, I could feel the cage calling me back to captivity. I could feel myself shrinking as the old familiar thoughts of not being enough, not being seen, and not being heard crept into my mind. In my head, I heard the familiar narratives of old neural pathways: *I don't have anything to offer this group. They are all so much sharper than I am. I'm getting old. I'm an imposter. I don't belong in this group of women. I shouldn't have come.*

I wasn't super close with all the women there, so I didn't confess to the group. When you're close to someone, it's the best move. But as soon as I got into my car, I began to tell God, out loud, what I was feeling. *Lord, I felt like I was a total loser back there. I'm getting old, and I feel . . .* and I proceeded to name all the things I was thinking and feeling. When I got home, I called a close friend and told her the same thing. I confessed my struggles to her, though it's still not an easy thing to do. I felt weak and ashamed that I still struggled with these petty issues at this point in my life. Later that night, I also told Dave.

I wasn't looking for their pity or even their affirmation. I needed to tell them because doing so is a dynamic trio; that is, when I tell Jesus, my husband, and a friend, the chances of me getting back into that cage again are usually a big fat zero!

You know how it is when you're trying to fall asleep in a hotel room and your eyes start playing tricks on you, making your suitcase or a coatrack look like a knife-wielding intruder? If you lie there long enough, you can freak yourself out. But there's an easy solution—turn on the light. Suddenly, what appeared scary is revealed to be nothing but your outfit for the next day hanging on the bathroom door. In the same way, the light of my confession immediately lit up the shadows of my past thought patterns.

Did I continue to struggle? Yes, that's what it means to be human. If we're breathing earthly air and not heavenly air, then we're still struggling to fully breathe. But did I get back into the cage? No. I continued living in the freedom I genuinely have. I wish these old emotional patterns and wounds would just go away for good, but I don't think they will until I die and leave them behind, once and for all.

But for now, this is where we are. Theologian Francis Schaeffer's famous question is more pertinent now than ever: "How should we then live?"[2] The answer is that we should live free, which means living in the light of honesty and confession. After all, "If we walk in the light, as he is in the light, we have fellowship with one another, and the blood of Jesus, his Son, purifies us from all sin" (1 John 1:7).

Much of what I've learned about walking in freedom comes from our friends Jamie and Donna Winship. Jamie wrote an extraordinary book about walking into freedom and into our identity in Christ called *Living Fearless*.[3] I have adapted some of Jamie's concepts for our reflection as we near the end of this chapter. To go even deeper into some important and biblical truths, I suggest you read his entire book.

Take a minute to ponder these questions:

1. Do you have a conflict in your marriage that cycles back continuously? What is it?
2. What are the deeper feelings you associate with that conflict (for example, I'm alone, my spouse isn't there for me emotionally or physically; I'm failing; and so forth)?

3. Ask God to silence any other voices but his, and then ask him to show you the first time you felt these things. (Perhaps a memory will pop up of something that happened when you were younger.)

4. Picture yourself standing in front of Jesus. (We use our imaginations all the time, so let's use them positively now.) Tell Jesus the lie you began to believe about yourself or about him after you experienced that memory.

5. Visually picture yourself handing the lie to Jesus. What does he do with it?

6. In exchange for the lie you gave him, picture him giving you something. He may bestow on you an encouraging name, place something in your hand, or give you what feels like a loving hug. For you, what will that be?

7. Thank him for taking the lies upon himself and for setting you free. Ask him to keep teaching you how to walk in the freedom he has given you.

DAVE'S REFLECTION

I have many regrets over the course of our forty-four-year marriage, but the biggest may be not understanding the depth of Ann's trauma that came from her family of origin. I underestimated how paralyzing the cage truly was for her.

Her dad and brothers were pillars in my life, and I saw them as strong men who shaped Ann in a positive and powerful way—and all of that was true. But I didn't realize how she felt regularly overlooked and wasn't told she was loved, at least not verbally. In addition to that, she experienced sexual abuse from people outside her family—it was the only time she was touched.

As Ann shared, I believed that our past and all of our pains were buried with Jesus, nailed to the cross, and "over and done with." I really didn't understand that these experiences—and the lies we believe as a result—go forward with us, eventually ending up smack-dab in the middle of our marriages. And the scary part is, if we don't deal with them, we will pass them down to our kids.

Early in our marriage, because I didn't understand how much Ann needed me to pour into her, I did not tell her often enough how much I truly loved her. Also, I rarely touched her unless I was interested in becoming intimate. I did not love her "as Christ loves the church" because I was selfish and lazy. Because she projected such a strong and capable persona, I honestly thought she was "all good."

I was wrong.

I learned that she needs me to love her daily with kind,

tender, and loving words. She also needs me to offer a consistently gentle, romantic, nonsexual touch. I am much better at it now, but it took me thirty years to even begin figuring some of this out. I'm telling you this because I hope that your husband will be open to reading at least this chapter of Ann's book so he can avoid spending years making the same mistakes I did.

So, men, if you've been brave enough to pick up your wife's book, please take heed of my caution. You have an amazing woman beside you who needs your tender yet powerful love and support.

See her.

Speak life to her.

Tell her you love her, and why.

Touch her tenderly and romantically (without sex as the motivator).

Keep doing all this daily until death do you part.

Trust me, your wife will come alive in ways you've only dreamed about. Why? Because you will be offering the love of God to her in a way no one else can. When we love our wives as Jesus loved the church, they grow into the women God created them to be—and we also grow into the men we were created to be. What a privilege and responsibility God has given each of us in marriage to bring out the very best in our spouse!

Don't waste this opportunity. Just a thought: Maybe you should put this book down right now and go tell your spouse how much you love her and what she means to you. You won't regret it.

CHAPTER 7

SPEAKING LIGHT INTO DARKNESS

Kind words are like honey—

sweet to the soul and healthy for the body.

PROVERBS 16:24 NLT

The mind is a deep well. In general, what we do or say cannot just flip on a dime. A fleeting desire to change usually changes very little. As we've learned, we have to do work—and keep doing the work—to learn the right ways to think, the best things to say, and ultimately what to do. Isn't this what we wish our husbands would do? Don't we hate it when it feels like he stopped trying to understand us in the ways he did when we were young and dating?

I remember the time on one of our first dates that Dave asked me deep questions all night long. He really wanted to know my heart and probed deep into my soul to draw me out. A few years later, I wondered what had happened to that guy—especially when he was watching ESPN for the third straight hour. He seemed to get annoyed if I ever wanted to "go deep."

These feelings of frustration may be valid, but they also show us that everything we've learned so far about our past affecting our mindset and present patterns must continue to be pursued. After all, our realities and feelings don't just go away. Emotional health is a lot like physical fitness: If we stop being intentional about it, it can fade quicker than we think. The concepts and strategies we've discussed need to be continually explored and reapplied until they become regular habits in our lives.

With this assumption in mind—that everything else we've covered is still being pursued—let's dive into the practical side of learning to speak life to our husbands and families.

WORDS: WATCHING AND WEIGHING

After the infamous boo story and God confirming in my spirit that I booed Dave, I felt God guiding me to pay attention not only to my thoughts about Dave but also to my words. It's all too easy to think that our words are just that—words. But they are so much more. The infamous playground burn that goes "sticks and stones may break my bones, but words will never hurt me" has to be the most unintelligent and inaccurate phrase ever written. (No offense to whichever nine-year-old coined such nonsense.) Like me, maybe you've realized that words can and have caused some of your greatest hurts and insecurities.

I was fifteen years old when I heard words that hurt me so deeply I can still remember exactly where I was and who spoke the words. It was a hot day in August, but I was full of excitement because it was picture day for the cheerleaders. I was a cheerleader for the first time, which was a huge deal for me, and I wanted to look my very best. After all, the photos were going to be posted in the football program distributed at every home game that year. In small-town Ohio, football was a *big deal* on Friday nights. I'd get to cheer with my friends in my coveted Findlay cheerleading uniform in front of a full stadium.

My mom dropped me off at my friend's house where we were going to get ready and then walk to where the pictures would be taken. As I had walked into the house, my friend's mom smiled sweetly and told me I looked cute. I beamed with pride as I joined my friends. We were all excited and nervous as we inspected our faces and hair, sharing mirrors. We finished preparing and walked outside, and I realized I had forgotten something in the bedroom. I told my friends to start walking and I'd meet up with them. I slipped back into the house and went into the bedroom, where I spotted my forgotten item. As I picked it up, I overheard my friend's sister say to her mom, "I can't believe you told Ann she looked cute when she came in the house."

I froze in my tracks, realizing they had no idea I was there. I felt a pit begin to form deep in my gut as their conversation continued. "She is soooo ugly!" I stood paralyzed in front of the mirror, fighting to take a breath. In hopeful anticipation, I waited for her mom's response to make it all not true. But the pregnant pause only brought more pain as she said, "I know, but she tries her best."

It felt like someone had punched me in the gut! Pain, shame, and embarrassment enveloped my entire being. I never used to really think much about my looks, but now I took one last look in the mirror and all I could see was, "Ugly! So ugly!"

Somehow I managed to sneak out of the house unnoticed and caught up to my friends, who had already begun posing for the pictures. I smiled, chatted, and did all the things they asked me to do, but the entire time, all I could hear in my mind was, *I am soooo ugly!*

As I type these words, it still brings tears to my eyes for the fifteen-year-old young woman who had no idea who she was, no idea who Jesus was, and no idea how to break free from words that wounded so deeply! I carried this story inside me for years, believing I would never tell it because it was too painful to share. The culture feeds women lies that our identity is found in our appearance. Just look at all the TV commercials, social media posts, and billboards. From a very young age, we are told what is beautiful. It makes me shudder as I consider the young women today who are beaten down by the random and cruel criticisms of social media. No wonder we have a mental health crisis in our country today. Now we're not just overhearing harsh words from one person; we're reading them in real time from loads of people.

Maybe cruel words have been spoken over you by someone you know or by people who hide behind the false safety of small screens. We've all faced it. Words from others inflict so much damage. But here's another truth: We also inflict much damage on ourselves by the words we speak over ourselves. And of course, the same rings true for the words we say to the people we dearly love who reside in our homes.

Words are rarely just words. As we've learned, they contain the very "power of life and death" (Proverbs 18:21). But why is this the case? How can a few syllables pack such a wide-ranging punch? Words are so extremely powerful because they are directly connected to the heart. For instance, you know how sometimes you're not sure how you feel about something until you've talked it out with someone you trust? That's because words reveal your heart, oftentimes even ahead of your thoughts or feelings. Jesus himself agreed: "For the mouth speaks what the heart is full of" (Luke 6:45). Chuck Swindoll says, "We need to think of our tongue as a messenger that runs errands for our heart. Our words reveal our character."[1]

Astoundingly, the reverse is also true. Our words also affect the content of our heart. Scripture teaches, "From the fruit of their lips people are filled with good things" (Proverbs 12:14). Tim Keller expounds on this truth: "Words embody and strengthen thoughts. When you say, 'I hate you. I wish you were dead,' you say it because you feel it. But afterward you feel it more because you said it. What you say fills your heart."[2]

But in our modern society, we tend to evaluate the content of our hearts in any given moment by what we feel in that moment. We say things like, "My heart just isn't in it today," or "The heart wants what it wants." We believe that our feelings or desires reveal our hearts. Of course, to a certain extent, they do. Our innermost thoughts and emotions certainly show us something significant about what's going on in our hearts. But what is overlooked in our modern obsession with feelings is that our words are more accurate indicators of the true state of our hearts.

You may be thinking, *But what about those times when I*

don't say exactly what I'm feeling on the inside because I'm trying to keep the peace? I don't feel better; in fact, it feels like I'm not being true to my heart. Yes, this can be the case. It can feel fake to not say what you feel. But all of this shows that we tend to believe our feelings are the purest reflections of our hearts.

But what if we try to think about it differently? What if by holding our tongues or speaking kindness in spite of our negative feelings, we reveal a more accurate reflection of a changed heart because it shows our ability and willingness to exercise self-control, patience, and humility? What if Swindoll is right that our words reveal not just our feelings but our character as well?

The world teaches us that everything we feel emanates from the heart and must eventually be expressed with words. Otherwise, we're being inauthentic and fake. There are slices of truth in such a viewpoint. Confessing our struggles and frustrations is something we should do as a regular practice. My point is not to hide from our feelings or fake the way we communicate. Rather, I want to show how we should unclip ourselves from the belief that feelings are the most accurate reflection of what's going on in our hearts. They just aren't; words are.

By their very nature, feelings can be fleeting and fickle.[3] Of course, feelings should not be ignored or invalidated, but neither should they be completely trusted at face value or, worse, allowed to be the master of our lives. We must remember that not saying every single thing we feel in every fleeting moment we feel it doesn't mean we're denying our hearts; it's living wisely from the heart. James takes it much further: "Indeed, we all make many mistakes. For if we could control our tongues, we would be perfect [also translated "mature" or "complete"] and could also *control ourselves in every other way*" (James 3:2 NLT, emphasis mine).

We would control ourselves in *every other way*—just from our words? Isn't that a bit much, James? This passage exposes our modern observation that words merely reveal our feelings. On the other hand, God's ways show us that our words are much more than random, purposeless synapses firing this way and that with every roving, random feeling we have. No, our words are a mirror that reveals what's going on in our hearts, no matter what we feel. If you're wondering if your heart is in the right place in a particular relationship or issue, searching your feelings will help, but feelings change so often and are so diverse that it's hard to nail them down. However, a quick evaluation of your words will offer an immediate and accurate answer. Is your heart right? Well, what are you saying (or not saying) on a regular basis? Are your words defensive, angry, or fearful, or are they kind, patient, and confident?

If we connect this truth with what we've learned so far about neural pathways and waking up to what's really going on inside our own internal worlds, especially in moments of stress, it all makes perfect sense. Our lives are not as siloed as we may think. What we say is a reflection of the deepest parts of us—and yes, what we choose *not to say* is also a reflection of the same. Our most authentic selves are expressed through the words we say—or those we don't say when we could have said them.

The implication is profound. When we work on our words, we work on our hearts. In much the same way that opening our wallets to give to someone else in need causes us to become more generous persons, opening our mouths to speak life to those around us causes us to become godlier persons—and consequently, less depressed, more positive, and more contented persons as well. It's one of the secrets hidden in the plain sight of Scripture: "Kind words are like honey—sweet to the soul and healthy for the body" (Proverbs 16:24 NLT). Positive words do more than just reflect feelings; they affect the soul and even the bodily health of the one who receives them. But they also do the same for the one who speaks them.

As I thought about the storm of words that swirls about among married couples, I realized that my words were less like raindrops and more like lightning strikes. I began to pay closer attention to the opportunities I was missing to use this power for Dave's benefit—and yes, also for my own. I began *watching and weighing* my words as much as I was *watching and waiting* for Dave to mess up again. And just as Scripture suggests, more than my language changed; my heart changed as well.

LITTLE BIG THINGS

When I first set out to speak life rather than shout boos, it took quite some time for my old neural pathways to be rerouted. Of course, I still have days when my old ways try to pull me back into negativity. That is just a fact of life. The battle for control of our minds and our words never ends. And make no mistake, it is a battle. But it is worth the fight.

As my thoughts about Dave began to change, as well as my methods of dealing with my own past and expectations showing up in my present, the right words came easier over a long period of time. I began to not only remember but also reimagine the marriage I was hoping for.

When we walk in hope instead of in despair and the strife of constant negativity, this hope begins to spread within us and into others. For me, it began to move from my head and heart into my mouth, so that my words began to follow my beliefs. And of course, each life-giving word spoken strengthened my beliefs and my hope in return. It was like the miracle of the water cycle scaled down to my little life, perpetuated over and over inside me. It was a living echo of Jesus' promise that "the water I give them will become in them a spring of water welling up to eternal life" (John 4:14). It no longer felt like I had to grab a bucket and strain to pull up positive things; it was like a new spring was bubbling up within me.

I began to want to communicate in a way that would uplift those around me. And it all started with allowing new hope to water these new desires every day, which turned into a new way of communicating. Ephesians 4:29 became a source of conviction and encouragement: "Do not let *any* unwholesome talk come out of your mouths, but *only* what is helpful for building others up according to their needs, that it may benefit those who listen" (emphasis mine). Words like *any* and *only* are straightforward and weighty, but they granted me the freedom in well-defined goals and boundaries beyond my feelings alone.

I now knew what my goal should be—to speak only what was helpful. And not in a way that was just helpful to me so I could get what I needed. Instead, it was a desire to speak what was helpful for building others up according to *their* needs, that it may benefit those who listen. Yes, I know the valid question we all want to ask: *But who will take care of my needs?* As much as possible, I encourage you to push pause on that question and stay the course on where you're going. You will get there.

As I took note of the way I had been talking to Dave for years, the little things proved to be not so little. For example, I seldom ever thanked him. I had a reason for this. Why would I thank him for something so trivial when I was doing everything for everybody and he was just showing up late at night? He was like a catcher in T-ball. In my mind I was the coach, the pitcher, and the groundskeeper. Besides, no one ever thanked *me* for doing all the things *I* was doing. I may have had some reasonable points, but this kind of destructive pride is never justifiable in the upside-down kingdom in which we live.

The good news is that this was a simple change to make. I just started thanking Dave for the little things he did, like coming home on time, taking the lead on the boys' nighttime routines, and helping me clean up the kitchen after dinner. I began saying things like, "Hey, thanks for grabbing the trash barrel and putting it away." Yes, I said it even when he would leave it by the curb for three days. I didn't say that part—again, this wasn't me denying my heart or reality. This was living out of a maturing heart that had come to realize that every single thought in my head, no matter how true, did not need to be said every single time.

Before my commitment to change my approach, I would have said something like this: "Really, Dave? It took you three days to bring in the trash barrel?" Or I would spiral into another internal mental tirade about how I have to do everything and always have to remind him to help out, which rarely works anyway. But I was beginning to learn that these kinds of reactions and thought patterns never led anywhere good.

Dave was already used to getting booed, so I tried to do the opposite of booing, with no disclaimers or strings attached. The crazy thing was, the more I thanked Dave for the little things, the more I was truly grateful for the things he did. And it allowed me to see more clearly and fully the husband I loved and admired so much. My words were changing my heart.

The little things began to lead to bigger things.

One of the main areas of our marriage that left me discontented and negative was my opinion of the way Dave should have been spiritually leading our family. Remember when we talked about expectations? Well, I had a laundry basket full of them. But now that I was beginning to acknowledge my own emotional narrative, I saw that much of what I was expecting from Dave was more a reflection of my own childhood pain than anything else. Yes, I still longed for him to lead, but I also needed to help. My method of motivating him wasn't working because life cannot spring forth from words of death. Only words of life can bring life.

Above all, I struggled with my view that Dave wasn't instilling spiritual depth in our family in the way I would do it. Maybe you've been there. Even if he tried, I was dissatisfied because he wasn't doing it my way. And sometimes I'd even compare him to another husband who was nailing it the way I hoped Dave would. Chop! Chop! However, as my awareness of my security in Christ continued to grow inch by inch, I began to accept that it was okay for Dave to not be me. He shouldn't be doing things exactly as I would because God had made him unique in himself. He needed to become the man God created him to be, not the man I wanted to create him to be. There is only one Creator—and he ain't me!

I realized I had a habit of using words like "you should," "you never," and "you always." Remember that these words give good boundaries when they come from Scripture and yet communicate unhealthy boundaries when they come from people. Many therapists and authors have warned against such language, so this idea probably isn't new to you. But I guess I had failed to get the psychological memo because if these were curse words (and they did make Dave feel cursed), I was slinging them like a pirate, complete with a little talking parrot on my shoulder who repeated them over and over again, just for good measure.

The truth is, these are the kinds of words that mothers say to young children: *You should finish your peas. You never put away your toys. You always try to skip brushing your teeth before bed.* Bad habits and behaviors or not, no man wants to be married to someone who talks to him like she's his mother. You can fight against this fact by pointing out all the ways your husband is acting like a child and deserves to be treated as such, but in the end, these kinds of words cannot produce good things among adults in marriage. They are shouts of boos in the first degree.

Even so, I was desperate, and Dave truly was missing the mark. So I doubled down on using negative words. In all honesty, my words were flat-out manipulation, intended to shame him into doing what I wanted him to do. "Hey, I had lunch with Paula today, and she told me that Steve *always* reads the Bible to their kids every night." It was a highly sophisticated form of nagging—and all Dave heard was "boo," mixed with a little spiritual shame and insecurity. But when I let go of this particular form of booing, it gave us all a chance to change. I stopped placing certain books on spiritual leadership on the table where he would see them. I stopped dropping not so

subtle hints. Instead, I tried God's way, which is to speak life
to the ones we love.

One night when Dave came home late, the boys were still
up. He went into their rooms to tell them good night and say
a quick prayer. Of course, he didn't do it the way I would have
done it. But instead of criticizing him, I asked the Lord to
open my eyes to what he was doing right in that moment. God
answered my prayer, and for the first time in our marriage,
I truly saw Dave's unique strength as a spiritual leader in our
home—and it was really less about what he said in his prayers
and more about his presence as a father.

When he came out of the boys' bedroom, I said, "I'm so
jealous of you."

He looked at me as if I had three heads. "Uh, why?"

"Because I'm here with the boys all day, and they hear me
talk for hours. But I watch you go in there, and they cling to
every word you say. You don't say as much as I do, but when
you say anything to them at all, it sinks deep into their soul."

His eyes were as big as saucers as I continued. "So I'm
jealous of that power you have." Then like a kid who doesn't
want to scare away a little squirrel, I slowly walked away so as
not to spook him any more than I already had.

I meant every word. I was learning to let go of trying to
control what Dave would or would not do, knowing I could
control only what *I* would or would not do. Dave was now in
God's hands, as was I. But guess where Dave went when he
got home the next night? Straight to the boys' bedroom. Soon
it became more of a regular practice—all because he wasn't
being nagged to spiritually lead our boys the way I wanted
him too. More than that, he was receiving my encouragement

because I could now see and affirm how he was leading, which made him want to lead more!

It has been one of the most significant moments of positivity in our marriage to date—and it came out of something that seems small and simple. God does disproportionate work, overwhelming our feeble efforts with divine outcomes, if we will only align ourselves with his ways, which really means we finally get *out of* his way.

If your husband is not leading spiritually in your home, and it seems he never will, as long as you know the right thing to do, do it. I know it's hard, but when everything seems to be up for grabs, stay the course, even if you don't seem to be reaping the rewards. Ask God to give you words to encourage your husband without making him feel like a failure. I know Dave would often feel clueless.

In our books *Vertical Marriage* and *No Perfect Parents*, we wrote about how Dave struggled growing up without a father. It's worth a read. Long story short, Dave had absolutely no model of how to be a dad, let alone how to lead spiritually—and he was a professional pastor! Your husband may also feel ill-equipped for the task at hand. Keep asking God for the best and creative ways to encourage your man as a husband and, if you have kids, as a dad. God loves to answer these prayers, and he will often use you as you speak words suited to your husband.

SKUNKS, KNIVES, AND WIVES

Earlier I mentioned that when we choose what to think or not think and what to say or not say, we are in a battle. Battle imagery may seem like extreme rhetoric, but the Bible actually uses the same language when addressing those swirling debates and thoughts inside us that compete for our attention and affections. In 2 Corinthians 10:5, Paul writes, "We demolish arguments and every pretension that sets itself up against the knowledge of God, and we take captive every thought to make it obedient to Christ."

While the primary context of this verse has to do with the early church's fight against idolatry, paganism, and heresy as the message of Jesus spread across the known world, we find principles here that we can apply to our patterns of thought and communication in marriage. Above all, Paul established the concept that certain thoughts need to be fought against to the point that they no longer have power over us. Literally, they should become our captives.

In chapter 6, I shared an illustration about a dog cage and how negative thoughts are the cage that hold us. Here I want to share a different cage illustration in which we take captive our negative thoughts and lock *them* up in the cage. Think about it this way. If you've ever had uninvited visitors in the form of skunks that slink under your porch or into your crawl space, you know you can't leave them there. Eventually, their presence will affect your whole home. So you call a pest specialist to bring a cage and take them captive.

In the same way, in our mental and spiritual lives, in our thought lives and patterns of communication, we have to take stinky thoughts and ideas captive. We must be willing to capture anything that wants to infiltrate and defile the spaces in which our families live and interact. It is a battle, to be sure, but deep down you know they are no match for you. If you want them gone, they have to go. The questions we explored at the end of chapter 6 can help us identify a particular negative thought and trade it with Jesus for something else altogether. Prayerfully, we can begin to take certain thoughts captive so that the right thoughts can take their place.

If we take the battle metaphor even further, we find Scripture meeting us there:

> A final word: Be strong in the Lord and in his mighty power. Put on all of God's armor so that you will be able to stand firm against all strategies of the devil. For we are not fighting against flesh-and-blood enemies, but against evil rulers and authorities of the unseen world, against mighty powers in this dark world, and against evil spirits in the heavenly places." (Ephesians 6:10–12 NLT)

Geez, Ann? I thought this was a book on speaking kindlier to your husband. Is the whole thing really this dramatic and serious? The answer is yes. I've already noted that there is an enemy of your soul who "comes *only* to steal and kill and destroy" (John 10:10, emphasis mine). But the good news is that you don't have to fight him under your own power. He has already been defeated, so his intentions for us are wrapped up in a losing battle, all because of Jesus' purpose for us as John 10:10 concludes: "that [we] may have life, and have it to the full."

Life that is lived to the full, both now and in the age to come, is Jesus' dream for each of us. He wants us to have it more than we want it for ourselves, which was why he was willing to die for us so we could possess it before we were even born. That should fill us with a sense of divine security, knowing we are loved in ways we can't even fathom. The dimensions of this love are measureless, yet God calls us to the glorious life of gaining more and more "power, together with all the Lord's holy people, to grasp how wide and long and high and deep is the love of Christ" (Ephesians 3:18). The power we gain over the course of our life in Christ—the power that helps us take our thoughts captive—comes from continually increasing our understanding of an infinite love that can never be fully measured and yet invites us to keep exploring its life-giving metrics.

Repeatedly exploring the love of God is a key to living our daily life in Christ. It is growing in a strength that is not our own, yet is fully extended to us in all things, including our thoughts and words. At the time of this writing, I am in my eighteenth year of reading the entire Bible through every year. I hesitate to share this because I know firsthand how such statements can spark feelings of shame, insecurity, or intimidation. My dear sister, that is not at all why I am sharing this. I don't spend this time desperately remeasuring the love of Christ because I am superspiritual; I do it because I am desperately needy. When I miss a few days of this time with him, I drift away so quickly. I become afraid, angry, and full of worry and complaining.

I have found that Jesus is my anchor, and anchors only work if you stay tied to them. He is my source of help. He is the one in whom I find hope. He is the only reason I am able to engage in battle and win because, he says, "Apart from me"—and I've been apart from him before—truly we "can do nothing" (John 15:5).

All this battle language conjures up another term of war—*surrender*. All religious-sounding terms aside, the easiest definition of surrender is this: giving up an opportunity to get your own way. Winning the battles for our marriages and families come when we live lives of surrender; that is, adopt a new way of being. We make a practice of letting go of our own desires in favor of God's. Giving up our own ways is not a popular concept, which is why the world is obsessed with fighting to never lose any right or preference whatsoever. We don't want to look or feel weak, so we resist anything that makes us feel not fully in control of our lives, even though our sense of control is an illusion. Real strength is rejecting the illusion that no weakness exists. Real strength begins with admitting weakness. When we are surrendered to Christ and his ways, we may look weak to the world, but in reality we become infinitely more powerful.

Another great word for *power* in this context is *influence*. Surrendered wives and moms may not have the most followers or likes, but they are the most powerful influencers in our society. We're the ones revamping the battles for our families. Our attitudes shift the very ethos of our homes. We alter our neighborhoods, communities, and churches by the power of our love and our kindness. Our power is otherworldly because when we are surrendered to Christ, we are also empowered by his Spirit.

If we are to do battle in this surrendered state, we will need other women who are willing to fight the right kind of war alongside us. We need girlfriends in which we can confide and who will demonstrate both empathy and wisdom in their responses. We need those who share our weaknesses to the point that they offer to pray with us more than offer us advice. We certainly don't need friends who use the power of their words to diminish our place in the battle, saying things like "He's an idiot," or "I told you not to marry him." I no longer have friends like that because I realized they weren't real friends in the first place. I do have painfully honest friends, but "wounds from [this kind of] friend can be trusted" (Proverbs 27:6). These friends share the same objectives and process, choosing surrendered lives before a loving Savior who is changing us every day, making us look, sound, and act more like him than we ever thought possible.

When we are living this surrendered, we become more aware of the power God has granted us. I began to realize just how insecure Dave could be. I stopped judging him for it and instead began trying to understand how hard it must be to carry that kind of weight all the time. My words have the power to give him life or to defeat him even further. Our friend, Stu Weber, writes, "A woman can so *easily* crush a man's spirit. With a look. With a word. With a shrug of indifference. . . . Her cynicism is utterly emasculating, and many times, incredibly subtle. Like a fine, thin blade it slices deep, penetrating to the very core of his masculine soul."[4] In the battle for our marriages, the last thing we should ever do is turn our weapons on the person we most need on our side.

Most women don't realize the power they have—and how easily their husbands feel the stab of a dagger, even when they didn't mean to use one. I have three sons, which means I am blessed beyond measure with three daughters-in-law. I don't think I realized the power I have as a woman until I began to see the influence my daughters-in-law have over our sons. My boys *love* their wives, and they each chose amazing women who are truly extraordinary in every way. They love my boys so well and so deeply, which is why they have so much influence in their lives, and rightly so. I can see how a certain glance can immediately change my boys' demeanors. It is a look I've given Dave many times over the years. Of course, the boys deserve it every time. And of course, their wives are quick to encourage and make sure they know they are loved and that everything is okay.

But it only takes a single look. That's some kind of power and influence—the kind intended for someone who fights and wins battles the right way. This power and influence have been given to you. Use it well.

SPEAKING LIGHT INTO DARKNESS

When God created the heavens and the earth, there was a specific moment when he "spoke" the lights on, forever separating the light from the darkness (Genesis 1:3). We are made in God's image, both male and female (v. 27). Though we can't speak and cause planets, animals, and trees to appear out of nothing, we do carry the inherited image of the Creator and the legacy of speaking light into dark places.

If we are to speak light, we must be able to pay attention to those moments when someone we love is stuck in darkness. In these times, we may have to overlook or delay the deserved correction that could be offered. We need to see them for who and where they are, calling out in them what the shadows of shame and doubt may be hiding from their self-awareness.

When I began to speak more life, Dave was not the only one in our home on the receiving end. I remember one night when one of our sons was a senior in high school. He came into our bedroom to tell us something. It was the spring semester, and he would soon be heading off to college to play football. I don't remember noticing any shadows within him, but for some reason, I felt compelled to speak light into him anyway. Before he left, I grabbed him by the shoulders and looked him squarely in the eyes. "Look at you," I beamed. "You are amazing in every way. Your leadership gifts are unlike any I've seen in people your age. You're going to go to college and going to be a man who influences many people for good, even if you don't even know it yet."

Honestly, he seemed fairly unimpressed. But that didn't stop me. I kept going. "When you speak, people are drawn to you, and God is going to use you mightily. And I cannot wait to see it happen!"

Finally he was like, "Okay, Mom. I get it. Thank you." You know, typical teenage boy response.

I kissed him good night, and he shuffled off to bed. But about a half hour later, he came into our bedroom, crying.

"What happened?" I asked.

"Mom, I'm not that guy. All those things you said, none of it's true!" Tears were falling from his eyes and plopping onto the floor. His face was flush with anguish.

"No, honey, I promise it's true."

He cut me off. "No, you don't know that I actually drank for the first time last weekend. That's who I am. You don't even know who I am, Mom." He continued to sob.

Now this was one of those moments when I definitely needed to surrender my own ways and deny speaking from my primary feelings. I wanted to set him straight about his poor decision. But when you're in a situation like that, the best move is to try not to freak out. Somehow I stayed calm and whispered a prayer to God for help in knowing what to say. Trust me, if you ask God to help in moments like these, he absolutely will.

I took my son by the shoulders again and said, "That may be what you did last weekend, but that's *not* who you are. All the things I said about you are absolutely true." His demeanor began to change. He became more peaceful. I could tell that God was using my words to strengthen him.

Thinking back, I wish I had also said, "And *this* is who you are. A man who makes mistakes, but whose heart always returns to the Lord. A man who is brave enough to admit to what he did. I've never been prouder of you!"

Now before you bring out the "Mom of the Year" sash and tiara, please know there have been many times I haven't responded in the right way. And what I wanted to say then was, "You're grounded for life, and I'm going to homeschool you through college and med school!" But my best strength would not display itself by coming down on him strongly; it would show up by being weak enough to let go of my momentary harsh instincts, which meant letting go of control so I could take hold of something better—powerful encouragement. The good news is that we're all already weak, so we're already halfway there. You don't have to be strong; you just have to surrender.

Finally, one more piece of wisdom on these kinds of matters. Let's go back to Ephesians 4:29, which urges us to speak "*only* what is helpful for building others up according to *their* needs" (emphasis mine). You know what I take from this?

It is *always* the right time to speak light into darkness. There will be plenty of time and opportunities for correction and conflict resolution. But when you find yourself in doubt (and you often will), no matter what it is, speak light into darkness. Speak truth. Speak love. Speak encouragement. Speak hope. Speak life.

Before we go any further, take a minute to go to our gracious God and confess to him all that you are feeling and thinking. I've experienced many days when I've had to repent over my many harsh words and attitudes. It's okay; just talk to God about it. Tell him the truth, which is the definition of confession. He sees you and wants the best for you and your husband.

DAVE'S REFLECTION

Wow, this chapter makes me tear up. As I hear Ann share the way she learned to speak life and light—and to fight in the right way to do so—I realize I am the man I am today because of the light she spoke into me. I know what you're thinking. *Shouldn't that be something you say about Jesus and not another human being?*

That's the crazy thing: I *am* saying it about Jesus! Ann was simply passing along to me the life that Jesus was passing along to her. He used her courage and strength, which to her felt like surrender and weakness, to shape me into someone I never could have become on my own. No one else besides Jesus could do that, and yet he has set it up so that his best work is done through the lives of people who put their trust in him.

To that end, our son to whom Ann spoke those words of life at the end of this chapter—he is now a pastor. In one of his sermons, he said, "When we see our spouse the way God sees our spouse, we will speak the words to them that God speaks to us—words of life, not death." How powerful it was for Ann and me to sit under his teaching and hear such truth, knowing the journey that God has taken him on.

I will also never forget the night that Ann told me she was jealous of my influence over the boys. Sometime later, I shared with her that this was a turning point for me. No, I didn't magically become "Father of the Year" overnight, but I did see past my insecurities to discern what my boys needed—and that God had put me there to help them with some of those needs. That's the thing about insecurity. For men, it can feel almost noble to walk in insecurity because it feels like we're honestly acknowledging our faults. We confuse humility with being withdrawn.

What's more, we don't want to make promises we won't be able to keep, so when we're stuck in that place of extreme insecurity, we just don't make many promises at all. And telling us we should be making more promises when we don't believe we're capable of keeping them simply turns up the pressure even more. We are more likely to emotionally disconnect than to risk failing at the connections we should be making.

But Ann relieved the pressure when she spoke truth and life into my insecurities. No, I didn't say all the things she would say, nor did I say them in the same way, but she let me know that it was okay to be the man God had made me to be. It was not okay to neglect my duties as a husband and a father, but it was okay to show up as myself, even if I was tired or weak, or not performing at my best in every aspect of being a husband or father. She called out who I was as a person, apart from my responsibilities and my performance in fulfilling them.

In Christ, I have been made for something good. I may haven't yet been the version of the person I was supposed to be (I'm still not), but by his grace, my presence still mattered. When Ann surrendered her standards of perfection, I was the one who was set free from my own cage of expectations. And when she took her thoughts captive, it took mine captive as well, freeing me from much of the negativity I was carrying so I could breathe and show up.

For men, just showing up is the hardest first step, but it's one we can more easily take when the woman who loves us most lets us know that it's okay to start showing up as we are, not as we should be.

CHAPTER 8

THE TENSION OF TRUTH AND LOVE

A gentle answer turns away wrath,

but a harsh word stirs up anger.

PROVERBS 15:1

I hope your heart is now open to pursuing a more affirming path lined with a whole lot less booing. Perhaps you've also begun to address your own well-worn mental paths that now need to be rerouted down healthier avenues. And I hope that the ways to communicate encouragement we've explored are starting to become your default way of being.

But as much as encouragement is good (which it is) and booing is bad (which it is), day-to-day communication in marriage entails dealing with some practical realities that do not fall into either of these categories. Sometimes there are conversations that need to be had that are super-complicated, overly detailed, or just plain hard. In fact, there are many times in a normal day of marriage and family life that *everything*—schedule conflicts, misunderstood words yelled across the house, crying babies, moody kids, sleepless nights, sick children, traffic jams, bosses making your lives miserable, extended family drama, financial woes, health scares and crises—hits the fan and difficult words need to be spoken. In these real, messy, complex moments of stress and pressure, how can we communicate in a way that doesn't sound like booing, either perceived or actual?

Especially as women, if we truly do know more than our husbands or children about what is going on in a certain situation, as well as what needs to be said, are we ever free to just say it? The answer is yes. We just have to approach truth telling by a different path than before. I had to learn this the hard way.

HOW WE WRAP THE TRUTH

I love Christmas. Who doesn't, right? The soft twinkle of glimmering lights. The rosy cheeks of little ones in their onesies and pajamas. The warm glow of a crackling fire. Hot cocoa in the afternoon light as a gentle snow falls outside the window, painting the family's memories with idyllic hues of cinnamon and gray. Great-aunt Janice's half-drunken claims to have fixed the engine of her 1954 Ford Atmos with just a simple bobby pin in the same year she built her house by herself with a tool belt around her waist and a baby on her hip.

You know, Christmas.

But for all of us kids at heart, the most exciting part of Christmas (yes, besides the birth of Jesus, obviously . . . please don't judge me) is the opening of presents. There is nothing quite like the visual of a fully decorated tree with so many presents scattered underneath that you can't see them all the way around. I know it is a blessed and privileged experience that not everyone gets to have, which is why I believe we should all do our best to help those in need have this kind of experience, and not just on Christmas. Why? Because everyone loves a good gift. After all, "Every good and perfect gift is from above, coming down from the Father of the heavenly lights" (James 1:17).

Even God likes gifts and lights.

The thing about Christmas presents is that we don't just put them out unwrapped for everyone to see. It would ruin the surprise. The anticipation of the gift is one of the best parts. So what do we do? We wrap the presents in decorative paper to keep the receiver from being able to ascertain the identity of their gift until the appointed time—at which, a mad dash of paper ripping ensues, rendering our living room floor littered with the best kind of mess.

Truth is a gift as well. Some might say it's one of the best. We've talked about the ways that the light of honesty with God, ourselves, and our husbands paves the path to thinking, speaking, and acting differently. When you live this way, "this light within you produces only what is good and right and *true*" (Ephesians 5:9 NLT, emphasis mine). But when truth is hidden, the light gets dimmer. Truth is connected to the light—to what is good and right.

The world at large also believes in the value of truth—well, at least they think they do. A quick search on Facebook, Instagram, or TikTok immediately produces a million well-meaning memes about the value of "radical honesty," memes saying something like, "If you can't handle me at my worst, then you don't deserve my best." It sounds nice, but I honestly and seriously doubt that anyone who has ever coined such a phrase was married for more than twelve to fifteen years. Why? Because marriage is a place where we absolutely see the worst in our spouse, and they see the worst in us. It's certainly not always memeworthy or noble-sounding. It can be discouraging. Deflating. Downright difficult.

It can also be true.

But speaking truth can bring down a marriage if it's not delivered with love and care. No one wants to hear unvarnished truth. It's too raw: *Your tone was so passive-aggressive. You absolutely looked that other woman up and down—with me standing right here. You said you were in the car on your way home, but you hadn't actually left the office.* I bet you can insert your own dialogue here.

You see, the world romanticizes truth because all people are made in the image of the One who is "full of grace and *truth*" (John 1:14, emphasis mine). We still want to eat from the tree that offers knowledge—truth, if you will—about good and evil. We want to know the truth about everything and everyone in our lives, and even those who claim not to believe in God or care about morality tend to become infuriated when they are lied to. Despite its proclaimed lack of religious scruples, the very essence of society's accepted interactions is still at least a shadowy reflection of the divine light that brought humanity into existence. We say we want to know the truth, but as Jack Nicholson famously shouted in *A Few Good Men*, "You can't handle the truth!"

The thing is, truth can cause more damage in marriage than lies. In fact, this is the reason some spouses begin to lie in the first place—they know their spouse can't handle the truth about their feelings, hurts, or resentments. It's a bad cycle, even in godly marriages. What a conundrum we find ourselves in! One of the most important gifts we need to give and receive can't be given and received without the same tears that our two-year-old has when she gets the wrong Barbie doll on Christmas morning. When the truth turns out to be different than expected, disappointment often floods in.

How do we give gifts at Christmas? We don't hide them, but we do *wrap* them. We put something else around the present, and so the truth of what they are getting is revealed in a way that honors, protects, and ultimately helps both the recipient and the giver. We have to do this in marriage as well. Hard truths need to be spoken. We need to talk about our likes and dislikes without shame, judgment, or retribution. We need to be able to share when we are offended or hurt, even if it seems like we're overreacting or being too sensitive. We need to establish boundaries for ourselves and acknowledge boundaries communicated by our significant other so that both can know and honor the respective limits of our conversations—and our life together.

These truths are gifts, but they typically can't just be given "as is." They can overwhelm or overpower the other person because, as we've learned, truth is a wonderful thing that can be hard to hear or accept at first. Like a medicine that helps our spouse overcome an illness, truth is potent and must be administered in measured doses.

Returning to our primary metaphor, we must learn to wrap truth before we give it to our husbands—and yes, they should learn to do the same toward us. If we're being honest, we can be guilty of wrapping and gifting truth to our husbands carelessly. Think back to everything I said to Dave in the days of the booing—it was all true! And I, along with billions of meme-watching, reel-loving people, instinctively believed that truth was *always* a good thing. After all, even Jesus was on board: "Then you will know the truth, and the truth will set you free" (John 8:32). I mean, he was talking about wives telling their husbands how poorly they were showing up or leading the family, correct? I'm sure that's embedded somewhere in the Greek, right?

My truth may have been accurate, but my wrapping was a mess, which left both Dave and me disappointed in the gift—because it wasn't at all what he wanted, and because I wasn't appreciated for what I had given. This kind of truth sets neither of us free. We both lost—and consequently, we both also lost sight of the truth, leaving us and our situation not only unchanged, but also worse than it was before. I've sat with thousands of women who can't figure out why truth telling doesn't lead to better marriages. They feel like a law of the universe has been broken.

The problem usually isn't the truth itself, though sometimes there are disputes about what is true. But the problem is often *the way* truth is communicated and perceived. Does any of this sound familiar: *You didn't have to be so mean. You know that I didn't mean it that way. Why can't you see that I'm trying? I said I was sorry, and it's like you're still mad.*

We've all been there. We don't need to hide truth. But we

do need to learn how to wrap it. Take heart. There is hope for all of us when it comes to gifting truth. God actually shows us exactly how to measure, cut, fold, and tape, helping us deliver the truth as the precious gift we intend it to be.

WHAT IS LOVE? (BABY, DON'T HURT ME)

The way to properly package truth is to wrap it in love. Now, before you roll your eyes and skip ahead to look for sections that are more practical and pertinent to real life, hear me out. This isn't some romanticized or religious-sounding answer that has very little bearing on or application to real life.

Again, most of us instinctively believe that speaking the truth is always an act of love. That's certainly what I thought, because again, I was functioning under the "delivering truth is always good" assumption of humanity's divinely breathed origins. I was mistaken.

Truth itself is always good, but the way we deliver it can actually be bad, as I just illustrated. Since the book of Proverbs leads us to value truth above lies in every situation, it goes without saying that "a gentle answer turns away wrath, but a harsh word stirs up anger" (Proverbs 15:1) is talking about answering honestly. We should never answer deceptively or manipulatively in order to preserve peace at the expense of truth. Instead, this verse indicates that there are ways to speak truth in a certain wrapping so that anger and hurt feelings are not stirred up in the exchange.

The phrase "speak the truth in love" comes from Ephesians 4:15, and it is one of the more commonly quoted verses among believers. But I believe it is misinterpreted more often than not. Again, this is because people consider truth telling to always be an act of love, overlooking the hundreds of ways in which Scripture leads us to wrap truth in something else before we throw it in someone's lap. To that end, the greatest gift of truth—literally, the One who is "the way and the truth and the life" (John 14:6)—came to earth wrapped in more than just swaddling clothes fit for a manger birth. The Word of God—his truth—came wrapped in "grace" (John 1:14). He didn't just start telling us everything we needed to change. Instead, he wrapped himself in our humanity, walking with us and sharing bite-sized morsels of divine truth as we continue our journey together.

Jesus not only tells the truth; he *is* the truth—and he not only tells truth in love; he *is* the truth in love. Therefore we can give up our own watered-down, memeworthy definitions of speaking truth in love and instead look at Christ's definitions of love. If we wrap our truth in these kinds of words, like Jesus himself, the truth truly can begin to set our marriages free.

Don't get the wrong idea—even truth beautifully wrapped in love can sting when it is opened. But if we wrap it properly, the love of Christ will cover a multitude of what we get wrong, bringing God's Spirit into the process and softening the hearts of both the giver and receiver.

If we're not careful, we can borrow more than just the world's working definition of truth, that is, "radical" truth telling every minute of every day in every way, no matter the timing, tone, or takeaway. We can also borrow the world's definition of love. We can interpret my "wrap the truth in love" comments as some sort of backward, matronly schtick for being a man's doormat and never giving our opinion because, despite their proclaimed might, men's delicate sensibilities and egos can't handle being told they may suck at doing dishes—or not doing them.

Love may be gentle, but it is not weak. Love may be tactful, but it is not withdrawn. Love may be patient, but it is not complacent. The world defines love as offering someone complete approval, agreeing with their viewpoint wholeheartedly and never questioning them—because doing so would break a newly formed sacred commandment of this world. This worldly commandment has been developed adjacent to the religious commandments the world labels repressive and obsolete.

The sacred commandment of the world is simple: Don't judge, that is, always approve, always agree, and never question. Trust me, speaking truth wrapped in this kind of love won't work, mainly because this wrapping isn't actually love at all. It is mutual enablement: *You tell me everything I think is right, and I'll tell you everything you think is right—and we'll keep telling each other that this is love.*

Real love, on the other hand, is well-defined in Scripture. We do not have to wonder about it, so we can also abandon whatever other versions we have adopted from this world's experiences or from our own broken stories. We can begin living out of God's story instead—and in this story, we don't always have to approve, agree, or remain unquestioning. In fact, real love requires us to resist each of these for the good of the person we love. You will have to tell them things no one wants to hear—how their pattern of harsh communication or action are hurting you, the family, or themselves and how their bending of the truth is breaking the peace in your home.

Remember, you are one of the pieces of iron that God has placed in this marriage, put here to sharpen another piece of iron. Sparks will sometimes fly, but when rightly defined love is applied to the process, both of you will be changed over time by both truth and love. That's how God set it up to work—and it works beautifully.

First Corinthians 13 is the simplest, most beautiful, and most comprehensive description of what godly love looks like. Yes, I know you've probably heard these words before. Please pretend you haven't. Don't look past the best thing on the menu because it's always been there and you're used to ordering something else. God's love is the original house-made special that always satisfies and never disappoints.

Real love is patient. When we speak truth impatiently, we may not be speaking it in love, which could well be why it isn't working. Real love is kind. When we say mean and hurtful truths without at least attempting to remain kind toward our spouse, the truth doesn't set them free; it binds them up in anger, resentment, and insecurity.

You may know parts of 1 Corinthians 13 by heart, but it is worth experiencing again and thinking through the ways each adjective can be applied as wrapping paper for the gifts of truth we need to give to our husbands and that they need to give to us:

> Love is patient, love is kind. It does not envy, it does not
> boast, it is not proud. It does not dishonor others, it is not
> self-seeking, it is not easily angered, it keeps no record of

wrongs. Love does not delight in evil but rejoices with the truth. It always protects, always trusts, always hopes, always perseveres. (1 Corinthians 13:4–7)

This description of love has a timeless, romantic effect on us, which is why it is so often read at weddings. But don't think this passage is mere fluffy rhetoric. In reality, it is super-practical. It provides a real-time filter for saying hard things to the one we love the most.

Before we utter a truth, can it be said in a way that shows patience, kindness, genuine humility, honor and respect, unselfishness? In a way that doesn't express anger? In a way that doesn't bring up all his past mistakes? In a way that isn't aimed at winning at all costs, but finds joy in mutual peace informed by truth? In a way that still protects him, trusts him, never stops hoping in him, and never gives up on him?

If we learn to speak truth in these ways, we will be speaking the truth in love. And yes, we have to *learn* to speak this new language of love, just as though we are learning to speak any new language. To do so requires effort.

I had a good friend who once told me she was growing weary of having to choose her words for her husband so delicately. After all, they had been married a long time—and it took so much work to carefully consider what she said. But after we talked a while, we came to the realization that most people at least try to choose their words with care when they are frustrated with a coworker or even a stranger on a plane. If this is the case, why wouldn't we take the most time to thoughtfully wrap our words for the most important person in our lives?

In the end, he is always worth the effort.

PLANTING SEEDS AND SEEKING WISDOM

So let's go there.

Oh, that's all I have to do? Geez, Ann, who can incorporate all of that into every hard conversation? Great question. On our own, certainly no one. And this is why the gospel is key to this entire mindset and process. If we believe we can learn how to speak divine life from the source of our human selves, we will fail miserably.

When you seek God's intervention in your conversations with your husband, you probably won't hear an audible voice telling you what to say, as though you're an FBI informant wearing a supernatural wire to a stakeout. That would be cool, but again, I'm very sorry. (And I'm also sorry to keep inventing these awesome scenarios and then telling you they'll never happen.) But when we lean into God's ways, we find God's whisper already speaking loud and clear—and this is no less of a miraculous intervention than a magical earpiece in your ear. For example, his voice in 1 Corinthians 13 teaches us how to speak the truth in love. You see, God is speaking to us now. It is miraculous. And listening is easier than you might think.

The more we meditate on these truths, the more we plant them and water them in the gardens of our heart, deep down where God's Spirit does his best work. No farmer holds up an ear of corn and says, "Look, everyone, I created corn." No, they understand and humbly acknowledge that another process beyond their control has been happening in unseen places underground. Without a seed—that is, a tiny piece of corn that no human created—farmers can never get a crop to reproduce itself in their fields. We plant and water life, but we don't create it.

Life change in our thoughts and words begins with something only God can do. We plant it and keep watering it day after day, which is what we're doing now. We read. We learn. We daily lean into God's ways, choosing them over our own patterns of thinking and speaking time and time again. We keep asking God for help—for him to do what only he can do in our lives and marriages. We watch and wait for God to cause the seeds (which he created and gave to us) to live and multiply. We plant. We water. But in the end, God makes it grow. After all, "It's not important who does the planting, or who does the watering. What's important is that God makes the seed grow" (1 Corinthians 3:7 NLT).

Why all the talk of corn and growing? Because it is crucial that we don't receive these kernels of truth and suddenly feel responsible for transforming our own lives, husbands, or marriages. That's a weight I know all too well, and the truth is, it will crush you. God's ways are an invitation to trust him to work in our lives. They are not edicts compelling us to get it right or else everything will go wrong. God is not a quid pro quo kind of Father—how dysfunctional would that be?

The Father's ways are not transactional; they are organic. Any farmer will tell you that organic processes are both predictable and unpredictable. You can expect certain things to happen—that is, plant and water, and you'll see something come up. But still, it is not a math equation. Rain, pests, drought, heat, changes in soil composition, and a hundred other variables can alter the timing or the outcome of any given crop in any given season. But even a bad season doesn't cause a farmer to throw up their hands and say, "This whole planting thing just doesn't work." No, they know there are unpredictable parts to it. Why? Because they are dealing with living things.

This is where expectation comes into play. Applying these principles to your marriage isn't a math equation. It works, but there will be bad weather and unforeseen pests (I don't mean your children, by the way) that will show up in every season of your marriage. Sometimes things get better. Sometimes you're holding on for dear life, just hoping there is something left at the end. This is why it's important to see the process as one that involves living things and doesn't guarantee static, predictable outcomes.

At first glance, God's ways may not always seem to work every time, which can cause people to become discouraged and give up: *This isn't working. You said if I spoke the truth in kindness, it would be well received.* The key here is the term *every time*. Marriage is not plug and play, and neither are you. Like the shifting seasons, God's ways in our marriages may not seem to work *every time*, but they certainly work *over time*.

It could mean years, not days or months. Yes, you may see a miraculous change in a week or two—God is good and powerful, and he can show up in incredible, often instantaneous, and tangible ways. But even the seeds that come from these moments must be replanted and rewatered in your marriage for the long run. This is what it means to follow God's ways, ways that are based in truth and love—real love defined by the One whose every essence is love. They keep producing life. And we are invited to keep growing more and more alive in this life.

Ah, what a relief to know that the life and health of ourselves or our marriages is something for which we are not ultimately responsible! We have a farmer's role, but not a seed's role. This realization should lead us to know that it's okay to not know what to do or say in every situation. If we're not the source, we can feel more at ease about feeling lost or confused, even if only in conversation. The bottom line is that we often lack the wisdom we need for knowing what to say—and as always, God's ways offer us direction.

James makes the path to seeking such wisdom clear: "If any of you lacks wisdom, you should ask God, who gives generously to all without finding fault, and it will be given to you" (James 1:5). The key to getting wisdom begins with acknowledging our need for wisdom. Imagine not having enough water for your crops, but not being able to admit it. If you want something to change, you have to acknowledge that you need it to change. You can't act as though you already have all the wisdom anyone could want and at the same time keep your heart humbly open to all the wisdom you need. If you don't seek more water, you won't get more water.

Thus, before we engage in certain conversations, we should seek God's counsel. We can begin with a simple prayer: "God, give me wisdom to know what to say and what not to say. Amen." You don't have to reinvent *The Book of Common Prayer* or paint something on the ceiling of the Sistine Chapel in order to pray effectively. Just talk to God.

When you pray, you may suddenly feel that you know what to say or not say, which is great. But just remember that God also sends and verifies wisdom by sources and methods other than our own internal feelings or impressions. Yes, you can "trust your gut," especially in kneejerk moments or situations. But perhaps a better phrase is "trust and verify your gut." Yes, I know it's not as pithy, but it may well be more helpful.

God offers us his life through his wisdom in three main ways: his Spirit, his people, and his Word. We've already addressed the first one. When you pray, listen for impressions in your heart from his Spirit. But also know that the best way to verify that it is the Spirit you're hearing is to make sure your experiences and impressions line up with trusted counsel from God's people and trusted truths from God's Word. When I'm especially emotional about a situation and my heart is involved, it can be hard to discern God's voice through his Spirit. We have to wait for confirmation and use wisdom in receiving it. My cute pastor, who is also my husband, has always taught that God speaks through the PEWS:

People—God will speak to us through our spouse, child, neighbor, or sometimes even a stranger.
Experiences—God will weave together our circumstances and experiences to speak to us.
Word—God often speaks to us directly through his Holy Word.
Spirit—God nudges us and impresses us in powerful ways through his Holy Spirit, who lives in each believer.

Seeking wisdom from God's people isn't the same as gossiping. Yes, you can vent. Yes, you can laugh. But in the end, share important things about your marriage only with those who share your beliefs and goals for your marriage.

Finally, if your gut feeling is not aligned with the plain principles of Scripture, don't trust it. I'm not necessarily talking here about passages about the roles of men and women in marriage and in church leadership—you know, the ones that have become ground zero for the battles and breakups in many churches, denominations, and friends. I'm not saying these things aren't important. I simply want you to know what I mean by seeking wisdom on what to say in your marriage by making sure it's in alignment with God's Word. We've already deeply explored this in terms of what it means to wrap truth in words the Bible defines as love.

God wants us to have his wisdom. He is not trying to withhold it from us, no matter how difficult and confusing our lives may be. Remember his disposition toward us: He "gives generously to all without finding fault" for asking because we don't know what to say or do (James 1:5). He is genuinely pleased by this request because it shows that we don't think we already know it all. It shows we are willing to adopt his ways of living in the tensions between truth and love because we know that merely saying what is true is not enough to set anyone free.

God's ways cause the truth to be heard more readily by the ones speaking it and hearing it. Of course, many people are skeptical about hearing when God speaks or even about whether he speaks at all. Know this, when you learn to recognize the ways he speaks, you can rest assured that he is a loving Father who wants you to hear from him. Don't be afraid to keep going to him and asking for wisdom. He will answer. It's who he is and what he does. What good parent doesn't want to communicate with their children? He loves you more than any earthly parent ever could.

I can't think of a better way to end this chapter than by praying together:

Lord, I really need your wisdom in knowing what to do and how to speak life to my husband and family. Help me wait on you before speaking. Help me hear you through your Word, your people, the experiences you allow in my life, and the whisper of your Spirit. I want to learn to speak this new language as I wrap my words in love. I ask that you teach me how to do it—and then how to do it again and again. In Jesus' name, Amen.

DAVE'S REFLECTION

Ann's wisdom on this topic revolutionized my thoughts on what it means to have hard conversations the right ways. If nothing else, the fact that she began taking the time to truly examine not just what she wanted to say to me, but also the way she was going to say it communicated love and respect. It made me feel like I was worth the effort of patience and nuance.

A friend once told us that words in marriage are like deposits into a safety deposit box. For years, Ann had been making deposit after deposit of criticism and disappointment. She thought it would motivate me and make me better, but all it did was get locked up inside the inner place of my resentment and insecurity. Any time a conversation began to go negative, I felt that box pulled out and more "truth deposits" of negativity put inside, painful reminders of my true insufficiencies as a husband, father, and man. It caused a constant tension inside me. It was truth, but not the kind that could set me free. Instead, it locked me up.

Then Ann began to live in a different kind of tension—one in which she moved away from seeing truth as something to be spoken apart from love. She stopped justifying and started approaching our conversations with a completely different attitude. Yes, I still heard hard things, but my value as a person felt like it was separated from the value of the issue at hand. Just because I was not meeting her expectations as a husband or dad no longer meant I was no good all around.

One of the reasons I can now hear Ann's words of truth is

that she has also been depositing so many words of affirmation. It is now the norm for Ann to compliment and affirm me for who I am and the things I do. I am not kidding—she does it every single day. But she isn't afraid to say the hard stuff. She still brings the heat, but it is much easier for me to receive truth and make changes.

It feels like we've gotten rid of the safety deposit box altogether. No one likes hard conversations, but I have stopped dreading them so much that I don't want to come home at night. I now trust that she truly loves me in spite of my faults. She sees that I am more than just the bad things I have done or the good things I am (or am not) doing. I now *want* more truth so I can grow.

And the thing is, her new pattern of living in this right kind of tension has made me want to do the same for her. No, it isn't quid pro quo. She doesn't do something to get something; neither do I. Instead she exercises courage in this area of our marriage, which has given me a safe path to follow her example and pursue growth for myself in all the same areas.

Trust me, it is much *safer* than any safety deposit box.

CHAPTER 9

THE WISDOM OF SAYING THE RIGHT HARD THINGS

A word fitly spoken

is like apples of gold in a setting of silver.

PROVERBS 25:11 ESV

In the classic early 2000s movie *The Sisterhood of the Traveling Pants*, four teen girls, each dealing with their own version of dysfunction and adventure, make a remarkable discovery. Though they vary greatly in height and weight, somehow a single pair of blue jeans fits each of them perfectly. To them, it is a mystical sign of their devoted sisterhood. So they set out on their respective journeys around the world, each agreeing to mail the pants to the next friend for their turn in a predetermined rotation, with a note describing how the pants had affected them.

This may sound strange, but in a way, we are in a similar situation. We're each so different—and that is more than okay. It is wonderful! We each face our own lives in this world. Our diversity is a beautiful reflection of the creative intentions of our wildly loving Father. You don't have to be exactly like me, and I don't have to be exactly like you. We each have a life that is a unique gift from God. This life affects the shape of our emotional selves, which affects the words we choose to use—or the words that feel like they choose us.

God's ways, however, fit each of us just right, even though we might think they never could. I have had the privilege of speaking to women all over the world and have been astounded at how we all deal with many of the same struggles. Yet God's principles apply to all of us. We are called to the same truths that inform our completely unique journeys. This is why we are invited to live our lives "trying to learn [by experience] what is pleasing to the Lord" (Ephesians 5:10 AMP). In other words, you and I each have to keep learning how these truths best work in our own marriages and according to our own unique personalities and inner ways of being.

I can't believe we're in the last chapter of our journey together in this book. I am cheering you on because I know you're committed to growing as a woman in Christ and as a woman who wants to speak life into everyone around you, including your husband.

This final chapter contains a few ideas I think are one-size-fits-all, so try them on for yourself and be encouraged on your journey beyond these pages.

"SHOULD I SAY IT?"

Maybe you're not a particularly positive person, or perhaps you're as sweet and gooey as a fresh cinnamon roll from the mall food court (okay, try to focus). The good news is, there are universal truths that fit each of us. We can also learn from others and grow in the areas where we are weak without downplaying those areas of our lives where we are strong.

If you are more of a direct communicator, which Dave calls "the Sermonator" type, you might share whatever comes into your head in a more forceful style. If your particular disposition is more docile and conflict-avoidant, then maybe thinking about some of the things we've been talking about is causing you to feel paralyzed, fearful that anything you say might offend your husband. If that's you, it's time to become more comfortable with your own voice in your marriage.

Perhaps you're somewhere in between, or perhaps you're more like me now—a verbal processor. I came across a quote attributed to nineteenth-century French novelist Gustave Flaubert: "The art of writing is the art of discovering what you believe." I'll take it one step further. For me, the art of talking also leads me to discover what I believe. If this is true for you as well, our first universal application in this chapter will probably hit you where it hits me—right between the eyes. Before we say something to our husbands, we should stop and quickly pray, "God, should I say it?" Can I just admit how stinking hard this has been for me to learn? I still struggle with it.

For those of us who have to say something to know if we think it, to pause and consider whether to say what came to our mind can be especially tricky. But for all of us, it's a good practice—and yes, for our husbands as well. It took me some time to really believe that every random thought in my head did not require verbalization in order to be known or validated. When you blurt out *everything* you think, there will be some things you've said that you will wish you hadn't. Your sentiments will be underdeveloped and perhaps not yet ready for consumption. They probably should have stayed in the oven a bit longer.

Over the years, I discovered that my verbal processing could short-circuit Dave's way of processing. I can be thinking out loud so much about my fears and my worries, about what could go wrong, or about what I'm not yet sure I'm upset with him over, that I don't even realize Dave has reverted to the fetal position in the farthest corner of the room. It's not that he doesn't care what I have to say, but everything inside my head may be too much for a pleasant pre-dinner conversation. And this tendency to think out loud isn't just a "woman problem." In fact, despite the stereotypes about women talking more excessively than men, I don't use as many words as Dave. I'm quieter than he is. But when it comes to something that needs to be processed, the words just tumble out of my mouth, passing through no filter on the way. I may not truly mean half the things I say in these moments, but they can still leave Dave feeling crushed.

The wisdom of Proverbs offers us insight into this problem: "Do you see someone who speaks in haste? There is more hope for a fool than for them" (29:20). *Ouch.* If you've read much in the book of Proverbs, you know that the writers have quite a bit to say about the fate of fools. To state that speaking hastily without thinking makes us more hopeless than the fool described in Proverbs is to adamantly declare that this is something we all should work on.

Furthermore, if we feel like we have to get everything out without giving the other party a chance to reply, we double down on foolishness. Marriage is rarely a good forum for monologues. I'm talking about those moments when you've fully said your piece for the past hour, to the point that only the sounds of your once internal but now external monologue are being heard. Maybe you keep cutting him off, even telling him what he really means, though he truly is saying something different. Proverbs again: "To answer before listening—that is folly and shame" (18:13).

I'm not saying that your husband shouldn't have to "bother" listening to your petty thoughts and feelings. No, sharing these things is a part of the lifelong vows we make. I only mean that we should be okay with knowing how we are made and how our husbands are made—and not be angry or disappointed that they are wired differently from us. Can you imagine if you and your husband were the same? You would either be so bored or so enraged that you would crush each other.

Wise inner work is learning how you communicate and becoming okay with the practice of taking pauses before saying everything that can humanly be said. After asking God if you should say it to your husband, you may choose to hold the thought for another time, or you may take it to your community first for more development or even correction. Or at the least, you may choose to limit what you say to only one or two of the thirty-seven points you have in your head, saving the full speech until after dinner.

These days, I try to make a habit of taking a conversation to God before I even engage my trusted friends about it. Sometimes I do this out loud, but sometimes I do it silently by writing in my journal. I have taken many walks where I purposely did not put my earbuds in so that I could talk to God about what I was contemplating. And guess what? He is always there—always listening. The peace that comes from seeking him first in these situations is astounding.

Yes, I know this may sound unrealistic, especially if you have babies or littles and you're just wishing you could be alone for five minutes so you could talk to God. I feel you and remember the challenges of those days. Over time, I found that my shower can become a place of holy communion with God. When we had babies, I also got into the habit of praying out loud in the car—my little ones didn't mind one bit.

Asking, "Should I?" also entails a sensitivity to what's going on in your husband's life. Yes, some things need to be said, no matter what else is going on. But other conversations can be delayed so they are heard in good faith, with time and grace to process. Remember the encouragement from Ephesians 4:29 (this may be a verse you memorize or stick on your fridge or mirror) to try to only say what is helpful for building others up according to *their* needs, that it may benefit those who listen. I often ask God, "Does this benefit Dave right now? Does it benefit me to say it? Does it benefit our marriage in this very moment?"

If it does, you can move to the next step. If it doesn't, maybe save it for another day—or perhaps you'll see it fade away on its own, meaning it wasn't as big of a deal to you as you thought. And since you stopped to ask before speaking, you saved you and your husband undue heartache.

"WHAT SHOULD I SAY, AND HOW SHOULD I SAY IT?"

If we conclude that our concern is okay to talk about, the next internal questions to God are these: "What should I say, and how should I say it?" which go hand in hand. This is related to the kind of wrapping we should use. With so much time and energy already being used up for your job, your children, your fitness, and a million other things, I know this can feel like you're putting a lot of time and energy into seemingly normal conversations. To that end, the main context here involves conversations you know can carry weight or spark confusion, dissention, or strife.

The idea is to ask God how your words should be spoken so that your husband can hear what you *really* want to say. You know what I mean, right? If you want to talk about buying something new and you say, "Hey, I know you're not making a lot of money right now, but I'd like to talk about getting a new car," your husband may very well focus on the part of your sentence that was less important to you. Can you guess which part? Yep, you pointed out the fact that he isn't making much money. I bet you've been there. Such questions of responsibility and security can cause intense emotions and reactions in anyone—shame, fear, anger, worry, irresponsibility.

You're no longer talking about a car because you're now in a heated debate about whether you have a problem with the amount of money he's making, or whatever else might have veered the conversation off course. To be clear, if you're honest with yourself, the same thing happens with things he says to you all the time. We all tend to interpret others' words through the filter of our own wiring and experience, to the point that certain spoken things will almost always suck up the most energy in the conversation.

If you've ever heard your husband say something like, "I wish you wouldn't have said that. You sound like your mother," you know what I mean. The ensuing conversation is now emotionally charged and focused on something other than resolving the issue of his objection to your choice of words. All this is notwithstanding the fact that your mother isn't even in the conversation, yet she somehow still looms large over the whole ordeal.

Being careful about what we say and how we say it is not manipulation. It is knowing and honoring the needs of your spouse—needs that may even be temporary in this moment or situation. Asking God how to wrap your words in a way that doesn't distract from the actual topic at hand and unnecessarily put your spouse on the defensive is just plain wise.

In the first scenario, your conversation would be more fruitful if you said, "Hey, I know you're working so hard and things are tight, and we can discuss this another time if you want, but I'd like to raise the idea about getting another car at some point in the future." In the second scenario, he could have just omitted or adjusted the second half of his sentence: "I wish you wouldn't have said that. Can we talk about it?" It's a significant difference when we choose an approach that considers the needs of the hearer, so that what is said benefits everyone involved.

This entire book has addressed how we should say certain things. We've also talked about asking God for wisdom when we don't know what to say. We can do one more thing on this front—ask our husband what he longs to hear from us. Obviously, doing this falls outside the previous scenarios based on actual situations. We can't rightly say, "Hey, I'm about to open a discussion about buying a new car. What exact words would you like me to use?" At that point, you've already used words.

No, this technique falls purely in the arena of encouragement and intimacy. It can feel awkward or inorganic to be so honest and direct. Again, we tend to want the right words to magically fall onto our lips, like in the movies. I've met many women who feel that if they have to tell their husbands what they like to hear him say or do, it somehow isn't real because he should have figured it out on his own. Direct honesty somehow diminishes the experience for us: *If I have to tell you, then what is the point?*

There is a better way to look at this kind of communication. If you are on a first date, yes, you pay close attention and even test the other person to see if they seem like a good fit with their words. You would certainly never say, "You know, Brad—it is Brad, right? I think I would really like it if you told me that you notice all the hard work I've put into picking out this restaurant for our date tonight." Yeah, that would be weird.

Marriage, on the other hand, is so much more than a consecutive series of first dates. The level of honesty in communication that would be awkward on a first date is not only acceptable in marriage; it is imperative. Vulnerability is the bedrock foundation of the marriage relationship. We put ourselves out there over and over again, knowing that the other person holds our delicate heart in their hands—and yes, men's hearts are delicate too, even if they sometimes don't realize it or admit it.

Marriage actually becomes deeper, sweeter, and more intimate when we learn to tell our spouse what makes us feel appreciated, wanted, seen, and loved. Yes, most people think it would be better if their significant other magically knew everything they want to hear on their own, but in actuality, it is our mutual vulnerability to talk about such things that makes the entire relationship truly deep and meaningful.

If you believe in soulmates, you may be surprised to know that even a soulmate can't read your mind, no matter what novels of Nicholas Sparks may portray. Real, healthy marriage stops treating the relationship like a perpetual first-date search for a psychic connection and more like a lifetime together to converse about anything and everything, including the things we like to hear in conversations. Trust me, it's more awkward not to ask and to spend a lifetime guessing the wrong answers. It may not make for the best love novel or rom-com, but it does make for a healthier, more fulfilling marriage.

When we started exploring this way of thinking, I asked Dave directly, "What are the top three sentences you would like to hear me say to you?"

With little hesitation, Dave replied, "I'm proud of you. I believe in you. I want you. I need you."

"Dave, you realize that's four sentences, right?"

He grinned mischievously, and we laughed together. This approach took us to a new place of emotional intimacy. And it wasn't awkward at all.

He then asked me the same question. My reply was also

easier than I thought it would be: "I love you and your voice matters. I see and appreciate all you do. I see you."

Of course, as we continue to grow over the years, the answers to such questions will evolve. In fact, the more we speak life to our husbands, the more the gaping hole inside him that longs for such love and affirmation will be filled. He will become increasingly confident in the fact that you are not only willing but also eager to meet his emotional needs, in alignment with Christ as the ultimate provider for both of you. Slowly he will begin releasing his tight grip on insecurity.

The thing is, as he speaks to you in the same way, so will you. You will begin telling each other new things you would love to hear your spouse say, taking you to new places of intimacy and adventure that your now healthy marriage has revealed over time.

"WHEN SHOULD I SAY IT?"

Vasili Alexandrovich Arkhipov may have saved your life, though I doubt you've ever heard of him, or of any other Russian submarine officer for that matter. On October 7, 1962, global tensions between Cuba, along with its ally the Soviet Union, and the United States had come to a dangerous boiling point. On that day, an American destroyer, the USS Beale, began dropping depth charges on the B-59, a Soviet submarine.

The B-59 also happened to be armed with a nuclear weapon.

The submarine's captain, Valentin Savitsky, had no way of

knowing that the depth charges exploding all around him were actually nonlethal "practice" rounds. In other words, they were warning shots, not an actual attack. But other US destroyers soon joined the USS Beale and intensified the barrage of depth charges around the B-59, intending to cause the submarine to surface, not to destroy it.

But as is often the case when we're in deep, dark places, Captain Savitsky didn't know the destroyer's intentions. Overwhelmed and exhausted, he wrongly assumed that the impending World War III everyone expected at any second had finally broken out above the surface. So he ordered the submarine's torpedo, along with its devastating nuclear payload, to be prepared for firing. The truth was, World War III had not begun, but Savitsky was about to inadvertently usher it in. The world as we know it could have been destroyed.

That's where Vasili Arkhipov comes in. The firing sequence for the nuclear torpedo required three officers to initiate. Savitsky and the other appointed senior officer agreed to fire the nuke, but Arkhipov refused. Despite the scary mess exploding all around him in dark places, he held on to the hope that there may have been something else besides nuclear war going on above the surface. It must have been a tense moment, but without Arkhipov's agreement to fire, the torpedo stayed in its tube, never to be fired.[1]

Sometimes we just need to wait. The world as we know it could be hanging in the balance.

If we return to the first question in this chapter—"Should I say it?"—the whisper I hear in my heart sometimes says, "No, don't say it." But more often, I hear, "Yes, you can say it, just not now." As Arkhipov's courageous choice highlights, the common expression "timing is everything" really doesn't do it justice. Timing determines the course of countless events and outcomes in our lives and relationships.

I suspect you have found yourself in Savitsky's desperate mindset before. I know I have. All hell is exploding around you and you assume all is lost anyway, so you might as well open your mouth and unleash the "nuclear option," finally dropping the obvious, dying-to-be-said bomb you know will blow to smithereens your night—or perhaps your marriage itself. You think to yourself, *It's probably already destroyed anyway, right?*

The temptation to *speak now* when instead we should *for now, wait* is one of the most powerful emotional forces we experience in this life. In moments of crisis, some of us are more wired for counterphobic reactions—that is, we would rather push forward and try to eliminate the source of the fear than sit in it with no foreseeable resolution in sight. Have you been there, the words you know you shouldn't say just dangling on the edge of your tongue? We just want to do it. Say it. Push the button. Bring the mushroom cloud. Find a release from the tension.

Let me love you well enough to tell you that there really is a time and a place for everything. If you're lost and disoriented in dark emotional or relational circumstances, it's probably the wrong time to fire off your verbal torpedoes and let the mushroom clouds fall where they may. The truth is, those clouds don't settle very easily. They can disrupt a whole society for generations to come—and so can words spoken in haste, which draws us back to the Scripture verse we referenced in chapter 8: "Do you see someone who speaks in haste? There is more hope for a fool than for them" (Proverbs 29:20).

But there is more hope than hopelessness!

Let me remind you of the central premise of this book: Our words can do more than cause destruction; they can also bring life. Words are like seeds—depending on what they are, there are seasons in which they should be planted and seasons when they should not. If you plant a good seed at a bad time, the outcome will still be bad. But if you plant a good seed at the right time, the outcome will be life. Scripture agrees: "Like apples of gold in settings of silver is a word spoken at the right time" (Proverbs 25:11 AMP).

When is "the right time"? There's no rule for this, which is why I encourage you to adopt prayerfulness as a lifestyle. This doesn't mean you have to spend an hour on your knees every time you need to talk to your husband about the finances or the kids' grades, though it wouldn't hurt. Scripture tells us to "pray without ceasing" (1 Thessalonians 5:17 ESV), which is not possible if we think of prayer only in terms of closing our eyes, getting on our knees, being quiet, or reciting a litany. To be clear, each of these are amazing practices, and we should do them. I only mean that there is no way to do all of them all of the time.

To pray without ceasing does not mean ceasing to do everything else in life. You can pray as you drive, so it is imperative to learn to do so without closing your eyes or raising your hands. You can talk to God all the time, even as you talk to others—you can pray in thoughts, whispers, quick "breath prayers" (a Christian tradition dating back to the third century), humming, or any other way you want. The key is being mindful and desiring to communicate with God. After all, he wants to communicate with you more than you do with him, so you can trust that he is there for all of the prayers, even the little ones squeaked out in moments of stress or frustration. And yes, even the little ones asking God about the best timing of your potential conversation.

While there are no rules here, there are principles. Try to pick a proper time. The moment your husband has just walked in the door from work or running errands and has yet to take off his shoes probably isn't the best time to drop a bomb (and vice versa). In moments of high stress, try not to say something that carries with it a potential for confusion or conflict.

In general, choosing to say something when both of you are really tired is also a bad idea. In my opinion, one main thing goes well in the marriage bedroom after midnight—and an emotionally charged conversation is not it. Again, you may feel like the bombs of daily stress over a particular issue are going off all around you, but it is still wise to assess the timing of your response.

As we come to the end, let's review the questions we can ask God to help us wrap our words in truth and love:

1. Should I say it?
2. What should I say?
3. How should I say it?
4. When should I say it?

We need to speak up about what is bothering us, but it is not a sign of weakness to ask when it's right to say it and wait for another time if indicated. It is a sign of wisdom. Speaking of wisdom, since this is our last chapter together, I've asked Dave to chime in a little earlier than usual with some wise reflections on our entire journey together.

DAVE'S REFLECTION

Ann has taught me so much about the timing of our words. I used to be more likely to blow things up in moments of stress, but we learned together that there is much more wisdom in asking God for the right words and the right timing to speak them. I still have a long way to go, and, yes, we still get into arguments. But with these principles more firmly in place than before, believe it or not, even our arguments are more helpful than harmful.

We have much to do to grow in these areas of communication and thinking, but as Ann has so eloquently shown us, it all comes down to be being led by someone other than ourselves. Ann talked about the person who speaks hastily having less hope for good outcomes than even the most foolish of people. In that same vein, Proverbs names another person who is in the same boat. "Do you see a person wise in their own eyes? There is more hope for a fool than for them" (Proverbs 26:12). This is the real crux of the matter of communication, relationships, and even life itself. Are we wise in our own eyes—meaning, do we truly believe that our way of seeing life is the right way?

I've been that fool before—truth is, we all have.

One of my favorite illustrations that Ann has used over the years comes from an antique tandem bicycle that hung in our garage for decades. When Ann was about twelve years old, she saved every penny for months until she could afford to buy it. It's old and needs repairs, but we like it just the way it is.

Ann loves to bring that old tandem bike onto the stage to talk about our need to avoid being wise in our own eyes by trying to stay in control of our lives. She begins by getting on the front seat, taking the bike wherever she wants it to go. We may not consciously name it, but it is human to instinctively believe we know what will bring us joy and fulfillment. We start pedaling and steering toward dating this person, chasing this dream, going to this college, or trying to make this particular relationship work.

As Ann has shared in her own life, we come to a rude awakening when we reach some of these goals and find that fulfillment doesn't flood in like we thought it would. We still feel lost and ashamed. So we make a new plan, turn the handlebars in a new direction, and keep pedaling forward in the direction of something or someone else. This cycle repeats every time we get somewhere we thought would fill up what is lacking inside. It is frustrating when even the one relationship we were sure would fulfill our deepest desires—marriage— also leaves us feeling disappointed and empty—not all the time, but enough times to make us feel the need to try to control our spouse.

This is usually the point where Ann shares how she came to know Christ after her sister came to faith and shared with her the amazing secret to life she had found. Ann became a Christ follower, but like most of us, she didn't really know what "following" Jesus meant. It was as though Jesus climbed onto the back of her tandem bike. After all, the bike did have an open seat for a passenger.

Then she did what we all tend to do. She did the steering of her life in the hopes that Jesus would add his incredible power to the pedaling. We are naturally wise in our own eyes, so when we think Jesus is pedaling wherever we want to go, we begin to steer in a hundred different directions under the illusion that Jesus will just make it happen.

Enter the idea of godly marriage. I mean, this is a wonderful goal to steer toward, right? Yes, so we steer in the best way we know how, but when we struggle to get there, we look behind us and say, "Hey, Jesus, what gives? I feel like I'm doing all the pedaling here. I figured this would be easier with you on board, but I'm starting to wonder." In fact, there are times when it feels like Jesus is actually using the brakes instead of pedaling us forward where we want to go.

Over time, however, we begin to hear Jesus whisper from the back seat on the tandem bike, "Hey, you should let me up front." It's hard to hear because we tend to be wise in our own eyes and think we already know the direction we need to go. After all, what could be godlier than seeking a "godly marriage"? The answer is this—letting God actually steer our marriage where he wants us to go, not wherever we think is right, no matter how much we go to church, read marriage books, or listen to marriage podcasts.

Ann loves to use the word *surrender*. Why? Because it entails letting someone else win. It means you are under their charge and give up control of where you will go in life. Over time, she realized that Jesus didn't want to steer her life because he wanted to control her as some cosmic judge and jury; he wanted her to surrender because he loves her and knows the best way to go.

Surrender is scary, but not as scary as steering your life in the wrong direction over and over again. Yes, this book talks about those moments when Ann woke up to the power of her words, but it was about much more than the words that she awakened to. It was a full surrender. She handed over control because she learned to trust.

Ann moved to the back seat of her tandem bike.

Don't let religious-sounding jargon fool you. Surrendering our words, marriages, and lives to Christ isn't a safe decision. Riding along with Jesus behind the wheel as he does the steering will take you to risky, scary, and awkward places. It will mean going to places you don't naturally want to go—forgiving your enemies, praying for those who use and abuse you, and sometimes losing arguments for the sake of winning peace. In these moments, we all tend to shout out to the divine One doing the steering, "Hey, this isn't where we want to go, is it? Are you sure you know what you're doing?" He always listens and his Word always speaks, but there are times when he doesn't explain the winding curves and blinding rains he steers us into. But now our role is no longer steering; it is pedaling. This means giving our continued energies to God's ways of thought, speech, relationships, family, and life itself.

Ann and I are both on this bike with Christ in the lead—it is a three-seat tandem on which we all pedal, but we now know that only one of us needs to steer. And there are so many times that we screw it all up, falling into anger, comparison, or frustration, but Christ keeps us from falling over. He maintains our balance by his grace, keeping us upright and moving forward. When we are so weak and tired that we can no longer pedal, his strength keeps propelling us forward.

The good news about having Jesus steer and pedal from the front seat is that our lives—the tandem bike—can keep going when we mess up and lose strength. Yes, even "if we are faithless, he remains faithful, for he cannot disown himself"

(2 Timothy 2:13). We will be corrected, but we will not be disowned. We will be led into new and sometimes difficult places, but we will never be abandoned. The one doing the driving turns back to us in our weakness and reassures us, "Never will I leave you; never will I forsake you" (Hebrews 13:5).

It is dangerous, to be sure, and yet it is the safest, most wonderful place we could ever be.

I love my wife, and I'm eternally grateful that God continues to use her to help me learn to let go of the handlebars and just pedal wherever he continues to lead us. Never underestimate the power that God has granted you in your marriage. It is not a power given to either the wife or the husband for the purpose of steering; it is divine power that comes from and leads to deeper places of surrender for all of us. It is a power that will reveal itself in thoughts and words. It changes things.

As Ann's life reveals, it has changed me.

CONCLUSION

Keep Speaking Life

What an incredible honor it has been to sit and talk with you in these pages! The subject has been a difficult one, but the takeaways are actually quite simple, though not necessarily always easy. But, hey, simple is better than complicated, right? As you keep leaning into God's leadership, surrendering to him in the everyday passing moments of life, I promise you will see more clearly whether or not to say something, when to say it, how to say it, and yes, what to say.

As a way to bringing all these ideas together from the last few chapters, let me tell the unforgettable story of the night Dave came home from a particularly long day and opened up the door for what could have been a particularly disastrous conversation. Remember, timing is everything, and when life's tensions are high and our bodies' energies are low, it is a wise idea to tread carefully with our words. It was a Sunday, so Dave had preached four services at our church that morning, after which he went and spent the day helping on the sidelines for the Detroit Lions game. Plus, he had led the Lions chapel service the night before. By the time he made it to our bed that night, he was running on fumes.

Yes, I had worked all day as well, doing the church thing, taking care of the kids he wasn't around to help with, and the like. These weren't realities to be ignored, but neither were they excuses for me to say anything and everything that came into my head. After all, I was no longer trying to steer; I was just pedaling and trying to follow God's lead and God's ways. God was beginning to truly change my thinking, helping me learn to pause and ask the right questions before speaking—though I knew I had much further to go.

Dave got into bed and inadvertently produced a verbal grenade, offering me the chance to pull the pin. "You know," he sighed in exhaustion, "I've been getting a lot of critiques lately about my sermons."

My mind perked up, even as my mouth said, "Huh, you don't say?" After all, as a perfectionist, I knew exactly all the ways Dave could do better, not only as a husband and a dad, but also as a pastor. I thought to myself, *Maybe if you would spend more time studying the Word, your sermons would be better. More succinct. More applicable. More theologically sound.*

Dave looked at me with those tired eyes, "What do you think? Am I doing an okay job?"

My finger was on the pin, but before pulling it, as I had done so many times before, I prayed a quick prayer in my heart: *God, should I say it? And if not, how should I say anything?* Dave had asked. I didn't want to lie. I had to say something.

Suddenly, thoughts flooded my mind from a place other

than my critiquing center. I felt intense compassion for my tired husband who had been working nonstop for days on end. I saw his heart to serve God and others. And I saw that he was willing not only to grow but also to be vulnerable with me. Could I have offered a five-page critique, complete with annotations and citations? Sure. Would I have been right? It might be easy to say yes, but thinking that I knew the definitive right conclusions about his work would have been nothing other than trying to be wise in my own eyes. We all know where that leads—nowhere good, that's for sure. Instead, I tried to follow the internal steering of the Spirit.

"I can't imagine what it's like to be you," I said.

His tired eyes perked up, "What do you mean?"

"Honey, you have thousands of people depending on you and watching your walk with God. What a weighty thing to carry! That must be so hard."

Silence ensued as Dave absorbed my words. A few minutes passed, and then he pulled me close to him in the bed, holding me in his arms. He whispered in my ear, "You are my life." The moment was so sweet and sacred that it still brings tears to my eyes when I think about it.

I hope that by now you know my heart. For every time I managed to follow the whisper of the Spirit into life and peace, there are a thousand other times when I blew up the moment with criticism and booing. There is no "wow, Ann really gets this." No, there is only "wow, God's grace for each of us is so big that if we will surrender, he promises to bring life into our thoughts, our words, and our marriages."

The truth is, I can't do any of this apart from Christ. Neither can you. But the good news is, we never have to be apart from him. We are free to keep growing in the art of transferring into others the life he pours into us. We can move past booing and into life-giving maturity. We can speak hard truths, learning to weigh the timing and ponder the wrapping. We can do this.

You can do this. Why? Because God is with you.

ACKNOWLEDGMENTS

To our son and literary agent, Austin—you are so good at what you do. We couldn't do any of this without your help and wisdom. Thank you! We are proud to call you our son and admire and love you so much.

John Driver—without you and your partnership, this book could not have gotten completed. You are so gifted. Thank you.

To our team at *FamilyLife Today*—we love you all a ton. Thanks for all you do to make the gospel clear and make us sound better.

Thanks to the team at Zondervan—you do your jobs with excellence. We have loved working with you.

NOTES

CHAPTER 1: ALL HE HEARD WAS "BOO!"

1. If you want to watch Ann and Dave tell this story, visit "'Vertical Marriage' Part 2: 'Boo!' Family Life hosts Ann and Dave Wilson," YouTube, September 12, 2019, www.youtube.com/watch?v=Nxr 37oQTGvk.
2. Max Lucado, *Just Like Jesus: A Heart Like His* (Nashville: Thomas Nelson, 1998), 4.

CHAPTER 2: STOP THE CHOP

1. To watch Ann talk about the chopping imagery, visit "Dave and Ann Wilson: Pruning and Cutting," YouTube, May 1, 2014, www .youtube.com/watch?v=7bY66X2KyzM.
2. The Arbinger Institute, *The Anatomy of Peace: Resolving the Heart of Conflict*, rev. ed. (Oakland, CA: Berrett-Koehler, 2015), 39.
3. This colloquialism, commonly used among physicians in residency, was quoted by neurosurgeon and terminal cancer patient Paul Kalanithi in his book *When Breath Becomes Air* (New York: Random House, 2016), 103.

CHAPTER 3: WHY DON'T *I* GET A HELPER?

1. Cameron Crowe, dir., *Jerry Maguire* (Culver City, CA: TriStar Pictures, 1996), multiple formats.
2. Kristi McLelland, "Jesus, Restorer of Women," *FamilyLife Today Podcast*, June 7, 2021, www.familylife.com/podcast/familylife -today/jesus-restorer-of-women.

CHAPTER 4: CHANGING THOUGHT PATTERNS

1. Ted Lowe, *Us in Mind: How Changing Your Thoughts Can Change Your Marriage* (Cumming, GA: Orange, 2022).
2. See "The Science of Love, with Dr. Helen Fisher | Big Think," YouTube, February 13, 2016, www.youtube.com/watch?v=0YP4n9G0qtQ.
3. See Ted Lowe, "Us in Mind: Change Your Thoughts, Change Your Marriage," *FamilyLife Today* interview, September 5, 2023, www.familylife.com/podcast/familylife-today/us-in-mind-change-your-thoughts-change-your-marriage-ted-lowe.
4. Lowe, "Us in Mind."
5. See The Arbinger Institute, *The Anatomy of Peace: Resolving the Heart of Conflict*, rev. ed. (Oakland, CA: Berrett-Koehler, 2015).
6. Arbinger Institute, *Anatomy of Peace*, 63.
7. John Gottman, "The Magic Relationship Ratio," YouTube, March 13, 2007, www.youtube.com/watch?v=Xw9SE315GtA&t=1s.
8. Gottman, "Magic Relationship Ratio."
9. "People Who Think Their Partners Are a Perfect Fit Stay Happier—Even if They're Wrong," Association for Psychological Science, February 28, 2011, www.psychologicalscience.org/news/releases/people-who-think-their-partners-are-a-perfect-fit-stay-happiereven-if-theyre-wrong.html.
10. Lowe, *Us in Mind*, 9.
11. "People Who Think Their Partners."

CHAPTER 6: GOING BACK TO GO FORWARD

1. This is the subtitle of Pete Scazzero's landmark book *Emotionally Healthy Spirituality: It's Impossible to Be Spiritually Mature While Remaining Emotionally Immature* (Grand Rapids: Zondervan, 2014).
2. The title of Schaeffer's seminal work: *How Should We Then Live? The Rise and Decline of Western Thought and Culture* (Old Tappen, NJ: Revell, 1976).
3. Questions below adapted from Jamie Winship, *Living Fearless: Exchanging the Lies of the World for the Liberating Truth of God* (Grand Rapids: Baker, 2022).

CHAPTER 7: SPEAKING LIGHT INTO DARKNESS

1. Chuck Swindoll, "Insights to Share: What If You Talk Too Much?," Insight for Living, accessed November 8, 2024, https://insight.org/resources/insights-to-share/individual/WIF-words-reveal-character.

2. Timothy Keller, *God's Wisdom for Navigating Life: A Year of Daily Devotions in the Book of Proverbs* (New York: Viking, 2017), 173.

3. Jennie Allen's amazing book on feelings deserves a full read: *Untangle Your Emotions: Naming What You Feel and Knowing What to Do About It* (New York: WaterBrook, 2024).

4. Stu Weber, *Four Pillars of a Man's Heart: Bringing Strength into Balance* (Colorado Springs: Multnomah, 1997), 269–70, italics in original.

CHAPTER 9: THE WISDOM OF SAYING THE RIGHT HARD THINGS

1. This story inspired the extraordinary 1995 movie *Crimson Tide*, starring Gene Hackman and Denzel Washington and directed by Tony Scott. See Edward Wilson, "Thank You Vasili Arkhipov, the Man Who Stopped Nuclear War," Nuclear Age Peace Foundation, October 27, 2012, www.wagingpeace.org/thank-you-vasili-arkhipov-the-man-who-stopped-nuclear-war/.

ABOUT THE AUTHORS

Ann and Dave Wilson are bestselling authors who have spent a lifetime in ministry inviting people from all walks of life into the vulnerable places of their marriage story of miraculous redemption. As leading voices for healthy Christian marriages, these retired founding pastors of Kensington Church now serve as *FamilyLife Today* radio and podcast hosts and nationally beloved marriage speakers. Dave was also the chaplain for the National Football League's Detroit Lions for thirty-three seasons. They have appeared on NBC's *Today Show* and a laundry list of other podcasts and media outlets. Ann and Dave have been married for more than forty years and have three grown sons, along with many grandchildren.